THE JEWS OF HOPE

THE JEWS OF HOPE

Martin Gilbert

MACMILLAN LONDON

ISBN 0 333 36625 5

First published 1984 by
Macmillan London Limited
London and Basingstoke

Associated companies in Auckland, Dallas,
Delhi, Dublin, Hong Kong, Johannesburg,
Lagos, Manzini, Melbourne, Nairobi,
New York, Singapore, Tokyo, Washington
and Zaria

Phototypeset by Wyvern Typesetting Limited, Bristol
Printed in Hong Kong

Contents

Contents

Illustrations

Illustrations

Preface

◇

In 1963 Elie Wiesel published his book *The Jews of Silence*. It was the story of the two and a half million Jews of Russia at a time when they had no possibility of emigration, no chance to practise their religion freely, and no foreseeable avenue of escape. During the twenty years that followed, the picture changed dramatically. The doors of emigration were opened. More than a quarter of a million Jews left the Soviet Union. Jewish cultural life revived, despite considerable official pressure. Preparations for emigration were continuous, and included for many Jews the study of the Hebrew language, of Jewish religion, Jewish culture and Jewish history. The Jews of silence became the Jews of hope.

As I write this preface, however, the possibility of Jewish emigration from the Soviet Union has been abruptly and drastically constricted. But hope, once roused, is not so easily destroyed.

This book is the story of some of those Soviet Jews whose hopes have been roused and whose Jewishness has been reborn, but who are now faced by the bleak prospect that they may never be allowed to leave, that their Jewishness will be crushed. It is a personal

Preface

account, based upon a journey, and upon conversations with a few remarkable individuals. For each story I have recounted here, many others could be told, reflecting similar activities, similar aspirations, similar suffering and similar courage. Other stories, which I should have liked to tell here, or people whom I should have liked to name, must, for the time being at least, remain untold, and anonymous.

One day, the history of the Jewish emigration movement will be written, and the part played by its leaders, many of whom are still not allowed to leave the Soviet Union, will be told in full.

Some of the Jews who have been refused permission to leave are keen to tell their stories. Others are reticent. But all of them are given added hope by the fact that visitors come, listen to their stories, and talk about them when they return to the West. These stories, and the debates among Jews in the Soviet Union today, are not the spreading of propaganda hostile to the Soviet State, but a natural discussion of problems, pressures and aspirations.

Cut off from the world, the Jews of hope refuse to bow down to superior force, or to accept the threat of never being allowed to leave the Soviet Union. A few are crushed by the pressures imposed upon them. Others are forced into silence and isolation. But most of them continue to struggle, against the odds, waiting for the day, which they continue to believe will eventually come, when they will be allowed to leave.

Merton College,   Martin Gilbert
Oxford
15 September 1983

1

On Culture Avenue

◇

A tiny suburban apartment on a top floor. A dingy
entrance way, a narrow stairwell, a slow, cramped lift.
On a quiet Leningrad evening the waste ground around
the apartment block is busy with young men and women
coming from every direction: drawing near across the
wide expanse of Culture Avenue, some arriving on foot,
others on board the trams that link Culture Avenue to
the city centre. Small figures in a vast landscape,
converging on this one stairway, pressing into this
particular lift, ascending to this single apartment.

It is Sunday, 17 May 1981. The affable Grigory
Vasserman is their host. A youngster still, at the age of
thirty, he has not yet aged with adversity. A teacher of
Hebrew, in a land where Hebrew-teaching is frowned
on, a religious leader in a country where atheism is the
rule, he knows the fear of a sudden police raid, of
uniformed militiamen pounding on the door, and of his
pupils forced to disperse into the cold night, their names
recorded for future reference, or for punishment.

This quiet Sunday evening is special. Those who are
gathering are filled with zeal for a distant anniversary.
Just over a week ago, on Saturday, 9 May 1981, the State

1

of Israel was thirty-three years old. On the following day, 10 May, militiamen sealed off a nearby apartment in which a celebratory meeting had been planned. On 17 May there is no anniversary, and there are no militiamen. But every one of those gathering in this Leningrad apartment has a special place in his or her heart for the anniversary of Israel's independence, for the Jewish National Home, for the land he has never known and the sky he has never seen, for the history of the Jews and their State. The meeting may be, of necessity, a week late. But for those who gather, it has lost none of its meaning.

The theme of this evening's gathering will be 'the relevance of the Jewish Sabbath'. A lecture has been prepared by Leonid Nilva, one of Vasserman's pupils. The apartment is filling up. Ten, twenty, thirty young Jews crowd into the bedroom, the kitchen and the hallway. The beds which filled the bedroom have been folded and stacked in the corner. The kitchen table has been set on its side. The hallway clutter has been piled up as compactly as possible, books lining one wall, coats and hats another. The tiny apartment has never been so crowded. But still they come: forty, fifty, sixty, until, when all have arrived, as many as seventy Jews are packed into that space, animated and expectant.

The meeting begins, if meeting it really is: more a throng bound by a theme. Israel is now thirty-three years old: the Israel to which so many in that apartment have applied to emigrate. For them, as Jews, Israel is their homeland. The Sabbath, around which so much of Jewish life is centred, will be explained and discussed. Now the excited voices fall silent. Someone is speaking, Vasserman or another, welcoming everyone to this gathering, this evening of learning, amid sorrow. But even the sorrow of exit visas refused is mingled with hope that one day the authorities will say 'go'.

The meeting has begun, the enthusiasm grows. The uncomfortable crush of bodies is no hindrance, but the reverse: a mass gesture of unity and faith. Israel exists two thousand miles to the south: and in this Leningrad suburb seventy Jews have risked the hostility of their rulers in order to share their Jewishness, and to reaffirm their Jewish national, spiritual, and cultural feelings. In their assertion of these feelings lies their strength. Emotions that in the West might seem old-fashioned, even naïve, are realities here, giving courage to an isolated people.

The lecturer, Leonid Nilva, begins his talk. The Jews fall silent. This is their culture and their heritage.

Suddenly there is a noise of boots in the stairwell. Fists pound on the door. The speaker's voice breaks off. The pounding grows. The door is opened. Four men enter: a uniformed militiaman, and three Civil Guards, in civilian clothes, with armbands. The four intruders seize books and papers, rummage in handbags, demand documents, and make lists of those present.

The four men insist upon seeing each person's 'passport', an identity card which every Soviet citizen carries. In each passport the name of the holder is followed by his date of birth, his place of residence, and then by his 'nationality'. In the case of more than 220 million Soviet citizens, this 'nationality' is given as 'Russian', 'Ukrainian', 'Armenian', 'Estonian', 'Latvian', or other national group. In the case of Jews, that 'nationality' is given as 'Jew' – *Evrei*. These Jews show their passports and have their names written down.

3

'Gathering here is no crime,' they protest. But their protest is in vain.

The seventy Jews are mostly men and women in their twenties and early thirties. One of them, Evgenia Utevskaya, is twenty-three years old. A year ago, her father Lev Utevsky received his visa and left for Israel. Her own visa application has since been turned down. She is filled with a passionate longing to be with her father, and with her people. As many more intruders now push their way into the apartment, she shows her passport, gives them her name and address, feeling a renewed pride, which the harassment only enhances, that she is a Jewess. Ironically, because her maternal grandfather was not a Jew, her passport describes her as 'Russian'.

Her passport handed back to her, Evgenia scans the street. A crowd has gathered, drummed up, as always in such cases, by the authorities. Its cries are clear, and vicious: 'It is a pity all Jews were not killed in the war,' 'Beat it out of our country.'

Evgenia winces. Would that she could 'beat it'. That is all that she has been asking for: permission to leave for Israel.

Inside the apartment an older man, Evgeni Lein, who has just celebrated his forty-second birthday, is determined not to allow this harassment to pass without protest. He is a Doctor of Technical Sciences. It was in his apartment a week earlier that the original independence day celebrations were to have taken place. Now, among the four intruders busy taking names here on Culture Avenue, Lein recognizes one who had been at his own apartment when it had been so effectively sealed off the previous Sunday: a large man, tall and

4

self-confident; now, as then, the obvious leader.

Evgeni Lein decides to act. He approaches the leader and demands *his* name. There is consternation. Questioning the authorities is neither approved, nor usual. Before he can repeat his question, Lein is seized by the arms, held tightly, and pulled, protesting, out of the apartment. He is under arrest.

Lein is taken by bus to a militia 'control point'; also taken away in the bus is Evgenia Utevskaya.

'Beat it, Jews, beat it,' chant the onlookers, under the unchallenged gaze of a dozen militiamen, and to the weary resignation of the Jews themselves. They have heard it all before, many times.

Lein is held at the milita 'control point'. The others are sent away. As Evgenia Utevskaya leaves, she sees two men in civilian clothes coming out of the building, and going up to a group of students. 'Listen,' one of the men calls out. 'We have to certify that a certain person was resisting arrest. We need two witnesses. You there, and you, will do!'

Two men step forward. The witnesses have been found. They give their names to the agents, and the students drift away. Evgenia Utevskaya hurries home to her apartment on Krestovsky Island. The episode is over. Culture Avenue returns to its accustomed calm.

———◇———

The affair of Culture Avenue has only just begun. While Lein is held in prison, and even his wife forbidden access to him, four other members of that Sunday's unfinished seminar are punished for their audacity. Semion Asch is sentenced to fifteen days in prison, and Tatyana Finkelstein to twelve, both charged with 'resisting the authorities'. Grigory Vasserman, the host of the meeting, and Leonid Nilva, the lecturer, are fined fifty roubles each – almost their monthly wage – for 'organizing an illegal meeting of a religious community'. The phrase 'religious community' is used in the charge because some of those present, being observant Jews, wore a *kippa* – a skull-cap – and because the lecture was to have been about the Sabbath.

Vasserman himself writes, laconically, a few days later: 'News from Leningrad is not much to speak about. A Jew, Grigory Vasserman, was fined fifty roubles for wearing a *kippa* and for speaking with his friends about Shabbat in his apartment. On the surface it is an unimportant event. You can laugh at the absurdity of it and forget it, but will that be enough? Events which are seemingly unimportant can, however, have grave consequences.'

Vasserman ends his letter: 'In medieval Spain, before lighting the fires of the Inquisition, the Church fined "impious" Jews and exercised other economic sanctions against them.'

Nilva challenges his fine, and denies the charge against him. The challenge is upheld by the court, and the money is refunded. Semion Asch, who suffers from a heart condition, is released.

Lein remains in prison. A trial is being prepared against him. He insists that he is innocent, that he struck no one. He demands his rights. The Soviet Constitution, he remarks, 'is very good: it is allowed to meet with friends'. He had pointed this out a week earlier, when his own apartment had been blocked. Now, in prison, he protests. Under the Soviet Criminal Code only very dangerous criminals can be arrested and imprisoned without warrant. Yet he, after a single alleged incident, has been taken away and locked behind bars, awaiting trial. His wife Ira, his nineteen-year-old daughter Alexandra, and his nine-year-old son Alex remain at home. Alexandra, a girl determined to live one day in Israel, prefers the Hebrew name, Nehama.

———◇———

Throughout the summer of 1981 Evgeni Lein was imprisoned in Leningrad, cut off from the world, denied visitors or correspondence. Only the Prosecutor appeared in person, to confront Lein with his crime: he had 'kicked' the militiaman during the incident on Culture Avenue. Lein insisted that he had not done any such thing, that in the crush and throng of bodies there had been no room to aim a meaningful blow, even if he had wanted to. The Prosecutor replied that it would be 'better' for Lein if he were to plead guilty. Lein repeated that he had not kicked the militiaman, that those in the apartment were far too tightly packed together for any such kick to have taken place, and that he had committed no crime. His protests were ignored.

Lein shared his prison cell with seven criminals: thieves, hooligans and thugs. The eight men had to make do with three beds: there was no space in the cell for a fourth bed. Lein, in search of a certain privacy, slept on the floor, under one of the beds, his face next to the lavatory pan. Although the conditions in the cell were no better and no worse for him than for the criminals, the attitude of the guards was decidedly worse. Lein, the Jew, was singled out for abuse and contempt. On one occasion the guards amused themselves by cutting off half his beard.

Lein remained in this prison cell for forty days. Then he was put in a cell of his own. No one was allowed to visit him: neither his wife and children, nor any of his friends. Repeatedly, he asked for a lawyer. But even this request was denied. Lein was alone. Outside his prison cell, Leningrad, city of rivers and palaces, glistened in the spring sun, and echoed to the admiring chatter of western tourists.

No one who has met Lein, as I have, can have any doubts about his courage. He is a man for whom adversity acts as a spur. In prison, and alone, he set about preparing his defence. Even to get writing paper, he had to apply to the Chief of the prison. And what then to write? The Prosecutor, calling again to see him, commented: 'You say you are not guilty. But think about your family.'

Many letters were sent to Lein, from Jews inside Russia, and from abroad, but none reached him. The psychological isolation, and the threat to his family, were greater torments than any physical pressure. How well the Soviet authorities know this, and how assiduously the KGB works to ensure that such isolation is maintained. It was they, not Lein, who were aware of the widespread concern at his arrest, and fate.

After fifty-three days in prison, Lein was at last allowed to see his wife. At the same time, he was told that his trial was to be held in two weeks' time. Both Lein and his wife demanded, yet again, the services of a lawyer. For ten days they received no answer. The trial was set for Wednesday, 5 August 1981. On the Tuesday, twenty-four hours before the ordeal, a lawyer appeared. His name was Denisovich. But his opening words left Lein in no doubt as to what the outcome of the trial would be. 'I see your case is falsified,' the lawyer told him. 'I cannot help you.'

While Lein tried to prepare his own defence, his friends made plans to attend the trial, knowing full well how difficult it would be to find a place in the courtroom. All were up early on that August day, but none as early as Lein. He had been woken up at four in the morning, and taken from his cell to what he later described, in his laconic way, as a 'special room'. It was more a cupboard than a room, without space to sit down. And so he stood, for eleven hours. No one came to see him. No food or drink was brought to him. Cramped, exhausted, hungry and parched, shortly before three o'clock that afternoon he was released from his torment and driven to the court.

An hour earlier, eighty Jews, most of them friends of Lein, had been admitted to the courthouse. With them were three American Jewish students studying in Leningrad, and two American diplomats, the Consul-General, Christopher Squire, and the Assistant Consul, Daniel Fried. All waited outside courtroom number eleven, where the trial was to be held: the same courtroom in which a year earlier a young Jew, Grigory Geishis, had been tried for draft evasion and sentenced to two years in a labour camp.

A few minutes before three o'clock, the doors of the courtroom were opened. In the rush to find seats the Jews were joined by many strangers, as well as KGB officials. Those Jews who managed to get in, squeezed tightly together on the benches. Some were allowed to stand at the back. Others, who were kneeling on the floor in front of the first row, or sitting on other people's laps, as well as the whole first row itself, were thrown out of the room. One, the Hebrew teacher Lev Furman, gave up his seat so that Lein's wife could remain in court.

As Lein was led into the courtroom, he saw that despite the number of strangers and KGB agents, about sixty Jews had managed to gain admittance. '*Shalom Chaverim*,' he said in Hebrew, '*Ani sameach lirot etchem*' – 'Greetings, friends, I am happy to see you.' '*Shalom*,' Lein's friends replied in unison.

It was rare for Jews to be given permission to attend such a trial. A further forty were standing, without permission, outside the courthouse. A few, prayer books in hand, were saying prayers at the courthouse wall. Among those who had managed to find a place in the courtroom was Mendel Geishis, whose son had been tried and sentenced in that same room.

'Many, many Jews gave support to each other during my father's trial,' Nehama Lein later recalled. 'It was dangerous even to be near the courthouse. But we stayed very strong. My father stayed very strong.'

The first clash came when the Judge asked Lein for his nationality. Lein replied that it was Jewish. The Judge asked why it was written down as 'Russian' in his passport. Lein explained that it had originally been Jewish, but that it had been changed to Russian because his father was Russian. Having become interested in what he called 'our history, our language, our culture', Lein wished, however, to change his nationality back to Jewish. To this, the Judge stated that one was allowed to change nationality 'only once'. Lein commented that earlier he had been an assimilated Jew. That was why he had not changed it then.

Lein was next asked whether he wished to be represented by an official court lawyer, or to represent himself. This led the Judge to question Lein as to why he was 'refusing' the services of Denisovich, the Soviet lawyer allotted to his case. Lein insisted that he was not refusing Denisovich. It was not that he did not like Denisovich, merely that he wished to conduct his own defence.

Lein's friends had known him as a quiet man. But as he defended himself, his strength was evident to all. One of those present at the trial commented: 'His appearance was Jewish: his black beard, his short, slight build. At times his hands shook, but his voice was always steady. The courtroom was hot and stifling. It was a very small room with few benches. Everyone was sweating and there was no room to move. But all our eyes were focused on Lein where he stood and sat.'

Lein now made two requests. First, he asked for his relatives to be allowed into the courtroom. Ira and Nehama stood up and said that they were present, as did Lein's mother. Lein then asked for his friends to enter, telling the Judge that he could see them through the courtroom window, standing outside. These were three of the eye witnesses to the events on Culture Avenue: Evgenia Utevskaya, S. Frumkin, and a third friend.

The Judge asked what concrete information these friends could provide. A guard was sent out. But at that point they were not brought in.

The Judge began to question Lein about the seminar of which the meeting on Culture Avenue had been a part. Lein explained that it had been a weekly seminar on 'Israeli history'. The Judge asked why, if this was so, one of the lectures had been on Spanish Jewish history. 'That *is* Israeli history,' Lein replied.

Lein then gave his version of what had happened on Culture Avenue on the evening of 17 May. The intruders had come in, he said, without showing any search warrants or other documents.

Asked how he knew the owner of the flat, Lein refused to answer. This he said was not pertinent to the charge.

The Judge then read out the charge. Lein was accused of assaulting a militiaman, Officer Semenov.

The first witness to be called was Semenov himself. A woman had approached him in the street, he said, and complained about noise. He had entered the apartment, with three Civil Guards, had shown a warrant, and had asked to see the documents of those present. When he had asked Lein for his documents, Lein had begun 'shouting, pushing his arms out', and had kicked him 'in the leg'.

The three Civil Guards were called. Their names were Yevseyev, Zhelobov and Yevdokimov. They addressed the court mumbling and indistinctly. But they confirmed Semenov's testimony. There had been a 'great deal of noise', they agreed, and 'many people'. But only one of them, Yevdokimov, said that he saw Lein strike the blow. The other two said only that they saw Lein 'leaning back in such a way as to suggest a kick would follow'.

One of the prosecution witnesses said how surprised he had been that so many people in the apartment, some seventy per cent, had their passports with them. There was sarcastic laughter from the audience. Soviet Jews, who know all too well that they may be questioned on such occasions, make sure that they have their documents with them.

Four witnesses then spoke for Lein. All were Jews: M. Khazin, T. Menaker, S. Frumkin, and Yakov

Gorodetsky. All stated categorically that Lein had not offered any resistance, had not hit Semenov on the leg, but on the contrary it was Semenov and those with him who had behaved in 'a provocative manner'.

Those present noticed that when these Jewish witnesses spoke, the court stenographer stopped taking notes. Later, in his verdict, the Judge was to comment: 'The court cannot trust the statements of these interrogated witnesses because of the fact that they had met often at the lectures and had known one another and Lein for a long period of time.'

As the case continued, the Jews who were standing outside the courtroom windows were chased away. Inside the courtroom the Judge was hostile to Lein's witnesses, but friendly to those of the Prosecutor. When the prosecution witnesses spoke it was, as one eye witness commented: 'robotlike and mechanical, as though their stories were memorized'.

At one point during the trial a militiaman took away the notes being made by Christopher Squire, the American Consul-General.

At five o'clock there was a break. When the court reassembled the Prosecutor demanded a three-year sentence. Assaulting a militiaman was a grave offence. Officer Semenov had been savagely kicked, leaving a bruise eight centimetres wide and ten centimetres long: a sizeable part of his left thigh. Lein demanded the medical document testifying to such a blow. A document was produced. It was dated twenty days after the alleged assault. According to the doctor, Semenov's thigh showed a residual scratch compatible with a blow struck twenty days before.

A fifth witness then spoke on Lein's behalf; the young

13

Jewess, Evgenia Utevskaya. With great courage she told the story of what she had seen outside the 'control point', of how the two KGB agents had approached the crowd, seeking 'witnesses', and of how they had then 'selected' two witnesses, neither of whom could possibly have seen the alleged assault.

Utevskaya's testimony caused consternation in the court.

Lein now spoke in his own defence. The Prosecutor, he said, 'was working for the KGB' and the prosecution had been mounted because Lein had applied to go to Israel and had attempted to learn about his Jewish culture.

Lein then denied the charge absolutely. There simply had not been room, he said, amid the crush of bodies in Vasserman's apartment, or in the hallway, or on the landing, for anybody to aim or strike a blow at anyone's thigh. The crush was similar, he said, 'to that in public transport during the rush hour'.

During his defence, Lein pointed out that there had been 'grave distortions' in the written charges relating to the case. It had been stated that the blow had been inflicted 'not in the hallway full of people, but out in the street, near the house. And, by the way,' Lein added, 'the wrong number of the house had been written. It was the number of the house where I *live*, and not where I had been *detained*.'

Lein also pointed out in his defence that neither the charge, nor the prosecution, had mentioned the type of shoes he had been wearing: soft shoes. With such shoes it was impossible, especially in such a crush, to strike a blow on the thigh 'resulting in a bruise measuring 8 by 10 centimetres'. It should also be noted, Lein told the

14

court, that Semenov had originally claimed he had been hit 'above the knee'. This he commented, 'was hardly the higher part of the thigh, as he had stated at the next stage of the investigation'.

Throughout the trial, Lein understood that his case had little to do with bruises, passports or a complaint about noise. He was being punished, he told the court in his final statement, because he and his family had wanted to learn Hebrew, to learn about Judaism and to go to Israel. Neither his arrest nor his imprisonment had changed his mind; nor would his sentence.

'I am innocent,' Lein declared. 'The circumstances of my arrest and the course of my interrogation obviously demonstrate that the prosecuting authorities adopted a biased attitude, and are preparing a reprisal against me and my family for our desire to know the history and language of the Jewish people, for our desire to leave the Soviet Union for the State of Israel.'

Lein then addressed the court once more in Hebrew: '*Yesh li tikva she' ani echeye b'Yerushalaim*' – 'I hope that one day I will be living in Jerusalem.'

Lein ended his defence: 'I demand my freedom,' and then he recited the lines from Psalm 43, again speaking Hebrew:

'Judge me, O God, and plead my cause against an ungodly nation:
'O deliver me from the deceitful and unjust man.'

Lein's recitation reduced the courtroom to silence.

The Prosecutor had demanded a three-year sentence to be served in a labour camp. The Judge sentenced Lein to two years 'deprivation of freedom'. Lein was to do 'work for the national economy', in places 'to be determined by the authorities'. Not forced labour, but labour. Not a labour camp, but work, and exile, in a Siberian city.

'It was a victory for us,' Lein later recalled. 'My friends were glad. It was a great joy.'

Lein and his friends knew that the two years' 'work for the national economy' would still involve hardship and humiliation. But the impact of the trial was considerable. The Prosecutor had been overruled. A young girl's courage had been manifest. A false charge had been held up to ridicule, and a harsh verdict shown to be absurd. Nor had Lein himself broken under the mental pressures of his two and a half months in prison, during which the Prosecutor had said to him, not once, but several times, 'You are alone. You are alone.'

Lein had confidence that he was not alone. During his trial it became clear that, as Lein phrased it, 'many men from abroad' had sent letters of protest to the Judge, and to the prison. These letters, Lein is convinced, had a 'very good effect': not a direct effect, perhaps, but certainly 'an indirect effect' on his sentence, on that courtroom victory which, in the months and years to come, was to give the Jews of Leningrad a feeling that all was not lost, that their request to emigrate might still, somehow, at some time, be granted.

For Lein, like so many of those who had crowded into the apartment on Culture Avenue, like so many of those who had crowded into the courtroom, was a 'refusenik', a Jew who had sought permission to emigrate to Israel, and had been refused. In Lein's case, he had first applied three years before. And now, as he was driven back to his prison cell, and as he contemplated the journey to

16

On Culture Avenue

Siberia, his chances of ever being allowed to leave the
Soviet Union seemed even more remote.

2

A pupil of a stoker

———◇———

Evgeni Lein's journey to Siberia, like so many prisoners'
journeys, was a nightmare. To this day he cannot recall
it without emotion. The special prison wagon attached
to the passenger train. His own 'prison' compartment,
designed for four prisoners but crammed with sixteen.
No room to lie down to sleep. A guard too lazy to
accompany them to the carriage lavatory, so that they
could not leave the compartment. The stench of urine.
Three days and three nights with only salted fish to eat,
and no water to drink for eight hours.

At their first destination, Sverdlovsk, Lein and his
fellow prisoners were put in a tiny cell, eight foot by two
foot, covered by a metal net, so crowded that all who
were in it had to stand. Only forty minutes exercise was
allowed each day. There was no outside window. The
electric light was kept on all day and all night. 'A million
insects fall down like rain.' The prisoners ate without
spoons, from an iron plate, 'like animals'.

For ten days Lein remained in prison in Sverdlovsk.
To keep up his morale, he wrote out Hebrew words, in
pencil, on an old cigarette packet. Then he was taken by
prison train for three more days, eastward to Achinsk,

where he was imprisoned for a further thirty days. Then the next lap by prison train, southward to the prison town of Chernogorsk, only 200 miles from the Mongolian border, but 3,700 miles from his home in Leningrad: further from Leningrad than Jerusalem.

The images of prison train, prison, and prison town crowd back as Lein recalls them. He is a gentle host, who seeks only to do what I can do whenever I please: to go to Israel. For me it is simply a question of choosing a flight and buying a ticket. For him, it is a dream which the authorities wish to turn into a nightmare – without an awakening.

At Chernogorsk, as Lein expresses it, 'I worked well, and got good marks for working well.' In the bizarre world of Soviet crime and punishment, Lein now entered upon the 'privileged' phase of his incarceration, 'work for the national economy'. He was allowed to live in a small wooden hut, and his wife Ira was given permission to join him there, leaving their daughter Nehama in their Leningrad apartment with the ten-year-old Alex. Ira made the 3,700-mile journey. She could bring books with her, and brought a suitcase full of legal textbooks. Lein studied these judicial books, and then, with the Soviet Criminal Code as his basis, wrote to the authorities to protest about his imprisonment.

Lein's persistence – some might call it cheek – was rewarded, and, to his own amazement, his sentence was reduced. It was a second victory. News of it spread rapidly through refusenik circles in Leningrad and beyond. From his remote hut, amid Siberian snows, Lein waited patiently for the day of his release. Just over forty miles away, he discovered, was the village where Lenin had been in exile in Tsarist days. Lenin's hut was now a museum, and a place of pilgrimage. But few, if any, from Leningrad, could make so distant a pilgrimage. Lein, with a characteristic twinkle in his eye, sought permission to visit Lenin's hut. Permission was granted.

So it was that Evgeni Lein, Jew, refusenik, Doctor of Technical Sciences, so-called criminal, travelled the short distance from Chernogorsk to Shushenskoye, and was photographed outside Lenin's place of exile: the outcast, and the hero.

Lein returned to Chernogorsk, and to the reality of 'work for the national economy': working as a draughtsman in a factory. He and his wife lived in one room of a wooden hut. While Lein worked, his wife spent the day searching for coal, food and water. A few vegetables might be obtainable, also a little fruit, and hard-boiled eggs. There was no meat and no butter.

The landlady of the room in which Lein lived was the proud owner of a television set. This she watched in the Leins' room. To their relief, the landlady was neither a drunkard, nor afraid, as so many landladies are, to take in lodgers who were under constant surveillance: 'the tail' as it is called.

There were times when the temperature at Chernogorsk fell to fifty degrees below zero. Lein's hut was heated by a coal stove, half of which was in his room, half in the landlady's room. The toilet was outside the hut, in the yard: a hole in the ground. There was no running water: all water had to be brought from a well some way off. Lein used an old-fashioned yoke to carry the water in buckets.

Food supplies were poor: one day while Lein and his wife were at Chernogorsk, a hundred bottles of milk reached the town. 'Almost the entire population of

A pupil of a stoker

74,000 rushed out to try to obtain some.' The milk was in any case very diluted, 'like white water'.

The weather in Chernogorsk was typical of central Siberia: windy, damp, with severe frosts, the ground swampy and treeless. Pollution affected the atmosphere. Alcoholism was endemic, life brutal and uncouth.

Lein worked well, and had to do so. For he was obliged each day to get the signature of his factory foreman, testifying that his work was satisfactory. Once a week he had to go to the Commandant's office, to obtain yet another signature, testifying that he had not infringed any of the conditions of his 'work for the national economy'. A single infringement, such as being late for work, and any chance of an early release might be ruled out, while several such infringements could mean a harsher sentence.

Each evening, Lein would try to study: Soviet law, in order to fight for his rights; English, in order to correspond and read more widely; and Hebrew, in order to prepare for life in Israel.

In remote Chernogorsk, Lein would repeat the words he used at his trial: 'I hope that one day I will be living in Jerusalem.' These words gave him strength.

In June 1982 Lein was released. His time in prison awaiting trial, and his successful appeal, had reduced his sentence to less than a year. So too, in his opinion, had western interest in his case. 'Your wife', he was told by a KGB official, 'wrote bad letters abroad.' 'How do you know?' Lein asked. 'I know all,' he was told.

'I am sure', Lein reflects ten months later, 'my release, it is the result of support of many people. They wanted to make it a criminal case. These letters and telegrams made it political,' and he adds, as he tells me his story, 'I

21

sit here and talk to you – it helps me.' 'It is not my story,' Lein adds, 'it is the story of Jewish life in Russia,' and his daughter Nehama interjects: 'It is an example for those Jews who will one day be in my father's position.'

Lein and his wife flew back to Leningrad on 6 June 1982. At about one thirty in the afternoon the aeroplane landed at the city's airport. More than fifty Jews were there to meet him: his son and daughter, many who had been at the apartment on Culture Avenue at the time of the raid, and others who had been in court during his trial. The plane taxied to the terminal building and came to a halt. Then suddenly its engines started up again, and it drove, like a car escaping from the scene of an accident, away from the terminal to a distant corner of the airfield.

'Why are we stopping here?' one of the stewardesses asked, of no one in particular. 'For what kind of sins are we here?'

Then, over the aircraft's loudspeaker, Lein was instructed to 'Leave the aircraft with your documents.' As he and his wife descended the steps, two men in plain clothes took them away 'in the special black car'.

'I thought I was arrested again,' Lein recalls. 'But they took me home.' Meanwhile, at the airport, 'my friends waited and waited and waited – with flowers'.

Among those waiting was Lein's daughter Nehama. As she watched the plane lurch into the distance, she feared, like her father, that he was to be arrested again. It had clearly been dangerous for the fifty to have assembled at all to welcome the released prisoner. But was he to be made the victim of their pleasure and excitement?

KGB agents approached Nehama and told her to

accompany them. They took her in one of their comfortable black limousines back towards the city. She assumed that she would not see her father again for some time, for months, years even. The limousine drove into the city from the south, across the canals and boulevards, over the Neva, past the Finland Station where Lenin had arrived in 1917 on the eve of the Bolshevik revolution, northwards to Lein's apartment on Engels Avenue. Despondent, she entered, and there, to her delight, was her father.

That evening Lein and his family were given a celebratory dinner at the home of a Hebrew teacher.

The two weeks after Lein's return from Siberia were a testing time for him. 'You must remember', one KGB officer told him, 'that you must have no meetings with your friends.' 'But', Nehama Lein wrote to a friend two weeks later, 'every day Jews come to us, and it's our victory.' A victory, yes; that was the widespread view of Lein's friends. 'But', Nehama commented, 'it's not freedom.'

Lein's experiences are the commonplace of a Soviet prisoner's life. Yet he added to them a dimension of protest which reflected his own character. What he did, however courageous by other standards, is disruptive and unacceptable in Soviet eyes. Nehama Lein understands her father's achievement – she is not without courage herself. 'They didn't like it,' she comments, 'when Soviet men know Soviet law – and begin to tell other Jews. The law is very important for us. There was one lawyer, a Jew, they told him to leave for Israel. He said he would finish his lectures. Then he went.' And then she asks, only to be disappointed by my negative reply: 'Are you a lawyer?'

The Jews of Hope

Since his release, Lein has again been refused permission to emigrate to Israel. In previous years, released prisoners would be allowed to go, would virtually be expelled from the Soviet Union. Now they are sent back to their cities, or to other cities, and still refused exit visas.

From his Leningrad apartment, a map of Israel on his wall, Lein corresponds with Jews abroad, keeping in a special notebook a record of every letter he sends, and noting any replies. But the majority of letters sent out by Lein, as by so many other Soviet Jews, never reached their destination. Nor do the majority of letters sent to them from the West ever reach them. Those letters that do arrive, and there are always some, are of great importance in maintaining morale, and contact.

Evgeni Lein, his wife and daughter are people of unusual determination. Lein is a man who refuses to remain silent, to sit still, to wait patiently for the day – which perhaps may never come – for his exit visa to be granted. He studies his law books at his crowded desk, and on his typewriter composes carefully argued letters of request and complaint to the authorities. He has nothing to lose. On the very day that he applied for an exit visa to Israel he was thrown out of his job as a mathematician, working with computers in the Cellulose Industry Institute. His wife also lost her job as a chemist. Both were out of work. Unable to get a new job, Lein faced a criminal charge of 'parasitism'. There is no unemployment in the Soviet Union. To be unemployed can be a criminal offence, punishable by imprisonment.

On his return to Leningrad in June 1982, Lein once more saw the spectre of prison before him. He knew that he could not be reinstated in his old job as a

24

A pupil of a stoker

mathematician, the job for which he was trained, and in which he had worked for several years.

Lein's demotion was not a unique feature of his case. The majority of refuseniks are permanently cut off from whatever work they did before they applied to leave. They are no longer accepted in their professions, and can no longer use their skills. But some work has to be found, however menial or absurd. Lein, in his inimitable way, protested to the authorities. 'Many Institutes are asking for mathematicians for computer work,' he pointed out. 'No,' he was told: there was no job for him. 'Then give me a simple job.' 'No, you have too good an education.'

Lein persevered, writing again to the authorities, citing Article 40 of the Soviet Constitution and Article 140 of the Soviet Labour Code. But even these legal guarantees of work for all were of no avail. Lein was told that as he had asked for a visa to Israel, it was impossible for him to be given a job.

For six months Lein wrote and argued. Meanwhile, he had reached the period when, still jobless, he was liable for criminal prosecution and prison. He made one final protest. 'And now,' he remarks triumphantly, 'I have a job – as a pupil of a stoker in a boiler house. I watch, and repair . . . .'

Lein works in the boiler house for eight hours each day. His earnings there are less than the official Soviet minimum wage, and scarcely cover the rent of his apartment. In the evening he has to work again, to supplement his income, and does so as a mathematics tutor, on a private basis. His friends help him out. 'If I hadn't the help of friends,' he says, 'I could not live.'

What does the future hold for Evgeni Lein, for his

family, and for his friends? 'I will demand permission to leave again and again,' he declares, his voice calm but resolute. 'Only a strong position is possible for me.'

Nehama Lein watches as her father speaks, proud of his recital, prompting him with her enthusiasm when his modesty intrudes. She too, in her early twenties, has felt the unpleasantness of a refusenik's situation. As a schoolgirl she was made to stand up in the middle of the class while the teacher announced for all to hear: 'Your parents are agents of Zionism.' She applied for an exit visa for Israel, in November 1977, on her own initiative. She was then sixteen years old. Her application was turned down. 'Why should foreign countries get your cheap labour?' she was asked. 'If you marry, your husband will also sit as a refusenik.'

Nehama's own job situation is critical. First she had to pass her final exam. But before being able to sit the exam she had to receive her teacher's formal approval, the 'control'. Her year's work was done, and done well. But each time she approached the teacher she was told, 'I am busy, I am busy, I am busy.' All the other pupils received the necessary 'control' and were given permission to sit the examination. Nehama was not. Then she was told: 'You didn't pass the exam. Out you go.'

Out she went, her hopes of training to become an economist ended, all chance gone of entering an Institute of higher education. She took whatever work she could. But wherever she worked she would be summoned by those in charge and told: 'Your father is a hooligan.' Her workmates became afraid to see her outside work. She became a pariah. Her 'crime' was to be both a refusenik, and the daughter of her father.

Even while her father had been in Siberia, Nehama

A pupil of a stoker

Lein braved the power of officialdom to champion his cause. On the first anniversary of his imprisonment she had prepared a party for some fifty of her father's friends and fellow refuseniks. That same day, a few hours before the party was to begin, the militia came to the flat on Engels Avenue and refused to allow Nehama to leave. When the guests began to arrive, they found the stairwell blocked. No one was allowed in.

Refused entry to the building, Lein's friends gathered in the open space outside and shouted up to Nehama, as she stood at the window: 'Shalom. How are you?' To which she answered, in all truthfulness: 'Bad.'

Lein smiles as his daughter tells her story. His is the look of a father who has reason to be proud. While he was more than 3,700 miles away, isolated from the world, unable to support his children, it was his daughter who carried the burden of struggle and survival. Yet her concern is for her young brother. 'I don't know what to do for my brother.'

Since that November day, Nehama Lein has been harassed time and time again. But in an unprecedented incident, some months before the affair on Culture Avenue, she and her father had sought the protection of the system, and obtained it. Nehama and her father were walking near their home when she was accosted by two men, and beaten up severely. Someone who saw the assault from the passing tram joined them in chasing after the culprits, seized one of them, and summoned the police.

The authorities tried to stop any trial taking place. The men had clearly been put up to the incident, and there was always the danger that a trial might expose them. But Lein insisted upon the men being brought to justice, according to Soviet law.

The trial took place. But the 'defendants' were not the men who had attacked Nehama. Lein at once protested that the wrong men had been produced. But the verdict was given as 'guilty'. The real attackers, whom many believed to have been KGB agents, were never brought to trial.

It was the sixth time that the child of a refusenik had been deliberately set upon in the street and violently attacked. But it was the first time that any action had been possible. Although the assailants escaped justice, the assault itself had been brought to court, and condemned.

Nehama Lein is proud of her father's action in pursuing the matter and bringing it to court. This too, in its small way, was a victory, of principle, if not of action. Soviet law, so often twisted against the refuseniks, had been used in their defence. From their position of weakness, there was a feeling of strength. It was perhaps this very victory, albeit partial, which had led the authorities to act against Lein on Culture Avenue.

———◇———

Lein continues to seek the right to leave the Soviet Union. On 17 May 1983 the 'conditional year' of his two-year sentence came to an end. He at once sent in a further visa application.

Having worked as an apprentice stoker since December 1982, in May 1983 Lein passed the professional stokers' examination, obtaining the 'second grade of skill' as a coal-gas stoker. This increased his earnings from 60 roubles a month to about 110 roubles. 'The weather is warm now,' Lein wrote in June 1983, 'the boilers are stopped, so I work repairing and cleaning the boilers and the boiler house.' Lein's application for a visa for himself and his family was again turned down in June 1983. 'So', he writes, 'on the 3rd of July we had a sad jubilee: five years from the day when we asked for the visa to Israel for the first time.' 'But', he adds, 'be sure, our spirit is high. We have been feeling a self-respect in the struggle for our departure.'

Lein realizes, as do all refuseniks at this time of 'nil' emigration, that his application to leave is unlikely to be granted. But, he writes, 'we are not afraid to repeat it again and again.'

Lein's fearlessness is reflected in his acts. First, throughout the spring of 1983 he fought, and fought successfully, for the right to receive letters and that his letters should be received abroad. Then, on 3 June 1983, he submitted a twenty-seven page petition to the Procurator General of the Soviet Union, A. M. Rekunov. In this petition Lein set out a total of fifty-six 'violations' of the Soviet Criminal Procedure Code during his arrest, imprisonment and trial. Lein's petition was rejected. But in its precise legal language, in its copious detail, and in its devastating revelations of injustice – of Soviet violations of Soviet Law – it constitutes an important milestone in the history of Jewish struggle in the Soviet Union.

———◇———

The refuseniks are not an organized group: in the Soviet Union no organizations are allowed outside the official ones. The refuseniks form nevertheless a band of brothers whose unity springs from their common adversity. Whether they are religious or not – and many of them are not – the Jewish festivals are for them a time of the renewal of strength and hope. Passover, with its annual message of liberation from bondage, echoes in their homes with its historic prayer, 'Next Year in Jerusalem.' Israel Independence Day is another cause for celebration. In April 1982 the Leningrad refuseniks had hoped to celebrate it by showing two Israeli films. A meeting place was arranged, as well as an alternative apartment in case the KGB were to learn of the first. But the plan misfired. Not only did the KGB surround the first apartment, but when the group tried to move on to their second venue, they were harassed and followed by the militiamen in cars, so that they had to abandon the evening altogether.

Elsewhere, the celebrations took place without films or demonstrations: private prayers and private longings.

Another moment of celebration is Purim, when Jews recite the Book of Esther, one of the most triumphant books of the Bible. Its ten chapters are a historical tale, not a religious one: God makes no appearance in it. Copies circulate among Soviet Jews like leaves of gold, its tale told and retold with deep emotion. Haman's wrath against Mordechai the Jew, who refused to bow before King Ahazuerus, is their own story. Haman reflects their own enemies. Mordechai mirrors the determination of their own leaders. Esther displays the courage of their own young women, like Evgenia Utevskaya and Nehama Lein.

The festival of Purim has a special significance for Soviet Jews, reflecting the historic time when the Jews 'had rule over them that hated them' and that month long ago 'which was turned unto them from sorrow to joy, and from mourning into a good day'. As children

A pupil of a stoker

don their fancy dress, the costume of Haman or the portrait of King Ahazuerus strike sombre chords.

For the Soviet authorities the gathering of children for their Purim play is an event to be stopped at all costs. In 1981, in Leningrad, an apartment was chosen for the celebration, and parents and children prepared to gather. The authorities had no idea of which apartment it was to be. They therefore blocked off about ten different homes.

At Purim in 1982 the Leins' apartment was one of those in which the festivities were to take place; festivities which can only take place in private homes, if they are to take place at all, for no hotel or Institution will make rooms available for such a purpose. Ten children were invited, crossing Leningrad in their fancy dress. But within minutes of their reaching Engels Avenue, five militia vans had drawn up outside the apartment, and some twenty-five militiamen sealed off the entrance. 'The children, they were afraid,' Nehama Lein recalls. 'There were about twenty-five men for ten children.'

In 1983 the Leins were once more would-be hosts to a small Purim party. To their surprise, and delight, five children managed to reach the apartment before the militiamen arrived. But then, once more, it was sealed off, and no more children could join the festivities.

The authorities in Leningrad do their utmost to interfere with Jewish activities, but they cannot destroy the will to celebrate.

3

On Police Bridge

——◇——

A young Jew with a large brown beard streaked with ginger, wearing a russet coloured fur hat, and carrying a russet coloured briefcase, stands in the snow at the corner of Leningrad's Nevski Prospect, where it crosses the former Police Bridge. His name is Mikhail Beizer, known to his friends as Misha. He is thirty-two years old.

Despite the cutting wind, Beizer stands on this cold corner, like a lecturer about to begin his class. Two men are with him, waiting for him to speak, as icy particles form in his beard. The young Jew speaks slowly, and with great earnestness. He is indeed giving a lecture, to this select audience of two – myself, and my friend Jonathan Wootliff, who accompanied me to the Soviet Union and who photographs the scene.

Not so long ago, Beizer was wont to lecture to groups of twenty or more. Recently the police have broken up such substantial gatherings, and have disconnected his telephone. The young man's subject is Jewish history: the Jewish history of Leningrad.

The story Beizer has to tell encapsulates the story of Jewish life in Tsarist Russia and after. With careful

On Police Bridge

erudition he speaks of an episode of nearly 250 years ago, an episode which took place on this very spot. For on this same corner, on 15 July 1738, a Jew, Borukh Leibov, was burned at the stake, together with Alexander Voznitzin, a retired naval Captain whom he had converted to Judaism. The burning of the two men, Jew and convert, had been ordered by the Empress Anna. Its effect was to revive Russian hatred against the Jews, and to justify further violence against them including, two years later, the expulsion of 573 Jews who, coming from more western lands, had found work or refuge on Russian soil. Nor did the expulsions end there, for in 1741 the Empress Elizabeth ordered all Jews 'of whatever calling and dignity', men and women, to be expelled. Only Jews who accepted baptism could remain. Ironically, Elizabeth decreed that these baptized Jews, while 'allowed to live in our Empire', were to be refused permission 'to go outside the country'.

By 1753, only fifteen years after the burning of Leibov and Voznitzin on the corner of Police Bridge, many thousands of Jews had been banished from Tsarist Russia: a contemporary account speaks of 35,000. But within forty years, by one of the recurring ironies of Jewish history, the children of these expelled Jews, together with hundreds of thousands of other Jews living in Poland and Lithuania, came once again under Tsarist rule. This happened with each of the three Russian partitions of Poland, culminating in the establishment by Catherine II in 1794 of a 'Pale of Settlement' in the western provinces of Russia in which Jews were to be confined: 'a vast territorial ghetto' as the historian Simon Dubnov has described it, imposed by law and maintained by decree. Subsequently, even this area was reduced, as Jews were driven out of hundreds of villages, out of the frontier areas – for security reasons – and out of many professions.

Misha Beizer is deeply versed in the history of his people, of their trials, tribulations and achievements. It was from this city, then St Petersburg, in 1825, that the Decembrists, hailed today in the Soviet Union as forerunners of the Bolshevik revolutionaries, challenged the severity of Tsarist rule. And it was one of the leading Decembrists, Paul Pestel, who proposed two possible and very different solutions to the problem of Russian Jewry. The first was that any future revolutionary Government in Russia should ensure compulsory assimilation and the end of Jewish culture. The second was that the Government-to-be should actively assist the Jews 'to form a separate commonwealth of their own'. Pestel suggested that this Jewish commonwealth should be somewhere in Asia Minor, 'an adequate area', as he expressed it, in which the two to three million Jews of Russia and Poland would, after crossing into Asia, 'form a separate Jewish State'.

A vision of Jewish statehood began, by slow and hesitant stages, to animate some Jewish thinkers. But from their capital, St Petersburg, the Tsars renewed the persecution of the Jews. This persecution was dominated and intensified by the pogroms of 1881: violent attacks on Jews and Jewish property which led to the immediate flight, within a single year, of more than 200,000 Jews to the United States, tens of thousands to western Europe, and 3,000 to Palestine. From then on, the exodus was substantial year by year.

There were some moments of hope, but they were few. One took place in 1882, as a result of a secret meeting in

On Police Bridge

a fashionable St Petersburg restaurant. Beizer leads us, Jonathan Wootliff and myself, to the courtyard of the restaurant itself. It is now part of a run-down apartment block on the Mojka canal. We gaze at what is left of the decor of a hundred years ago, as Beizer speaks of the day when a wealthy Jewish philanthropist had visited the restaurant in order to try to bribe one of the Tsar's leading anti-Semitic ministers, Nikolai Ignatev, to modify his proposed anti-Jewish legislation. As Ignatev pretended to doze after lunch, he was slipped a series of envelopes. In each was a substantial sum of money.

The restaurant bribe was not entirely in vain: the legislation was modified. But Ignatev's 'temporary rules' of 3 May 1882, known to the Jews as the 'May Laws', were harsh enough, forbidding any Jew from settling outside towns and hamlets, or from carrying on any business on Sunday or on Christian holidays.

Not only Jewish commerce, but also Jewish culture, were the object of Tsarist repression. On 17 August 1883, scarcely a year after the 'May Laws', the Minister of the Interior, Count Dmitrii Tolstoi, forbade the performance of all theatrical shows in Yiddish – then the language of most Russian Jews and, for the previous five years, the focus of a theatrical revival. Henceforth, until the revolutions of 1917, Yiddish performances, so central to Jewish cultural life, had to be performed illegally. Often they would be put on in the guise of 'German' plays.

Thus Jewish life in Tsarist Russia, then the home of more than five million Jews, proceeded with artifice and anger, the Jews and the authorities in a continual, yet unequal struggle. No decade was free from hazard or persecution. On 29 May 1891 all 20,000 Jews of Moscow were expelled, and 2,000 of St Petersburg's 21,000 Jews were deported, many of them in chains. Six months later, on 29 September 1891, the anti-Jewish pogroms began once more, followed by the second mass flight, to the United States, South America, South Africa, western Europe, and again to Palestine. In the single year following the pogroms of 1891, more than 100,000 Russian Jews left for America, followed by 65,000 during the next two years.

Persecution and discrimination continued: in 1892 hundreds of Jewish families were expelled from the Crimean town of Yalta. Already, in St Petersburg, Jews had been forced to indicate on their shops not merely the family name of the owner, but his first names and his father's names, 'with the end in view', as the law explained, 'of averting possible misunderstandings': that is, to make it crystal clear that the owner was a Jew.

The Jewish response to persecution took many forms. Some Jews assimilated. Some joined the revolutionary parties, committed to the overthrow of Tsarism, and to a Socialist or Marxist Russia. Others looked for their future to emigration, most of them to the United States, the 'Golden Land' of millions of would-be emigrants. A small band turned their hopes to emigration southwards, to Palestine, and to the building of a Jewish homeland far from persecution and prejudice. These 'Lovers of Zion' had sent their first small group to Palestine in 1882, when they helped to set up an agricultural village, Rishon le-Zion: 'the first in Zion', today a flourishing town.

A few Russian Jews succeeded in acquiring substantial wealth inside Russia itself. Beizer's tour of Leningrad includes short lectures on the steps of the former

On Police Bridge

palace of Samuel Poliakov, the railway builder, on the pavement outside the former banking house of Vavelberg, and in a courtyard – for there is a cold, biting wind – facing the house where Baron Horace Günzberg was born. Günzberg was tireless in his efforts to obtain the amelioration of the Jewish condition inside Russia. An opponent of Jewish emigration from Russia, he hoped that the Jews would be able eventually to participate in Russian life without being discriminated against.

As we walk along the boulevards of the former capital, Beizer describes how, in 1891, negotiations were conducted by the Jewish Colonization Association, with a view to settling 125,000 Russian Jews a year in special colonies in the distant Argentine. This scheme, financed by Baron Maurice de Hirsch, aimed at reducing the number of Jews remaining in Russia. It was a great philanthropic venture. But it never succeeded in attracting more than 13,500 Jews a year, far below the national annual growth of the Jewish population. The activities of the Association, however, were yet another talking point among Russian Jews anxious to find some way out of their dilemma.

All these matters were discussed from every angle in the journals of the time. One of these journals was *Voschod*, which had begun publication in 1881. Beizer has prepared for me a copy of the title-page of this hundred-year-old journal. Unfortunately, this harmless bibliographical item was confiscated from me at Moscow airport as I left the Soviet Union. It was only a sentimental gift, being readily available in libraries in the West: but it was judged subversive.

The articles in *Voschod* were typical of their time. It was an era, as Beizer phrases it, when Jewish intellectuals 'hesitated what to do and where to go'. The journal described, in its fortnightly articles, the activities of the Jewish Colonization Association in the Argentine, and of Russian Jews in Palestine. But it advocated neither assimilation, emigration nor Zionism: it sought instead to give the widest possible expression to Jewish cultural and national themes, to the debate itself.

Beizer's tour of Leningrad echoes with these debates of a past century. There seems no street in the city which does not have some Jewish association. A few paces from the spot where Leibov and Voznitzin had been burned at the stake in 1738, Beizer points out another historic site, the place where, after the Kishinev pogrom of 1903, a Jewish student, Pinkhas Dashevski, stabbed and wounded the Russian journalist, P. A. Krushevan, whose viciously anti-Semitic articles had stirred anti-Jewish hatreds in Kishinev for several years. 'Death to the Jews' had been the cry of the mob in Kishinev on 6 April 1903; forty-five Jews had been murdered during that day of looting, burning and rape.

For publishing details of the Kishinev pogrom, the journal *Voschod* was closed down; and for his attack on Krushevan, Dashevski was sentenced to five years penal service. Within two months of Dashevski's act of desperation on Police Bridge, the Zionist leader, Theodor Herzl, visited St Petersburg, seeking Tsarist support for a Jewish National Home in Palestine.

Dashevski's act had considerable significance for Russian Jews. It was, Beizer comments, 'the act of a Jew in a Jewish cause. Hitherto, Jews had acted in the cause of others.'

Much was now done by Jews in their own cause, cultural and national, religious and Zionist. But much

On Police Bridge

was also done by Russian Jews in the growing Russian political struggle. Jews were prominent in all the revolutionary movements of the time: Socialist, Menshevik and Bolshevik. When the Bolshevik revolution came in October 1917, individual Jews predominated among its leaders, and Jewish energies, which had so long been suppressed by Tsarist laws, contributed to the revolution's success. Among the sites on Beizer's tour is the former Leningrad headquarters of the Cheka, or secret police, forerunner of the KGB. It was in this building that a Jew, S. P. Uritsky, presided in 1918 over the work of imposing and maintaining Communist control in the Leningrad region. For a short time, one of Uritsky's assistants in this same building was the Jewish writer Isaak Babel, who ten years later was himself to become a victim of the terror.

Uritsky was assassinated in August 1918 by a member of the outlawed Left Social Revolutionary Party. As a result of the assassin's bullet, he became a hero in the Soviet pantheon. Almost all his fellow Jewish revolutionaries were to become victims of the system they had fought so hard to establish.

It is Beizer who has identified the link between this building and Jewish history. No wall plaques or guide books tell these stories. Hence Beizer's excitement at describing who had lived where, and which events had taken place in which building. His work of discovery has taken him several years of reading and delving.

The excitement of telling his stories seems to keep Beizer warm, despite the freezing wind and the ice particles which form in his beard. Seeking to avoid the cold, cutting edge of the wind, I persuade Beizer to move to a more sheltered corner. It is by the old Senate building, and there, in the relative shelter of a wall, Beizer speaks of the petitions that used to be sent to the Senate by Jews in provincial Russia, seeking the protection of the Tsar for their harassed communities. As he talks I feel even colder than before. The corner he has brought us to is covered with a solid pavement of ice.

As Beizer talks, I reflect on the fact that for many who have not met them, Soviet Jews may seem a people apart – strange, remote figures belonging to another world. But they are western Jews, trapped in time and space, but not in spirit. As I listen to Beizer talking, I wonder to myself, if his grandparents had left Russia as mine did during the Tsarist days, would he now be a historian at Oxford or Jerusalem?

For Jews in Soviet Russia, history is filled with echoes and parallels, some ominous, some inspiring. It is an integral part of their present story. Beizer's historical tours are confined to history. They have no political content. Even so, they were often shadowed by more KGB agents than there were participants on the tour. By the summer of 1982, Beizer says, 'there were twice as many policemen on my route as excursionists.' He had even been forced to cancel some of the tours after several of those participating in them had been summoned by the militia, and warned that such an interest in Jewish history was officially frowned on.

Twice during the three-hour tour Beizer, Wootliff and I seek warmth and refreshment in a small café. Beizer continues his historical explanations as we sit in the café, and in his enthusiasm he spreads out his historical papers, filling the whole table with documents. Wootliff takes several photographs of the intense look of the teacher, as he pores over a publisher's brochure of 1913,

issued in St Petersburg and announcing the works of
three Jewish authors, Theodor Herzl, the founder of
Zionism; Haim Nachman Bialik, the Hebrew poet; and
Vladimir Jabotinsky, a young Russian Zionist who was
later to be the founder of the Revisionist movement,
committed to mass immigration to Palestine, and full
Jewish statehood.

Wootliff photographs Beizer poring over the brochure
and explaining it to me. Unfortunately, all Wootliff's
photographs, and mine, were taken away at Moscow
airport as we were leaving the Soviet Union. They were
then developed by the authorities, and returned. But
more than two thirds, including all those of Beizer in the
café, were held back, and never returned. The copy of
the brochure which Beizer himself gave me as a gift was
also confiscated. No reasons were given.

Beizer has appealed to the authorities several times
for official permission to make his tours, or at least for an
end to police surveillance. Each request was in vain.
'The authorities are always polite', he comments, 'but
quite firm. "Everything is impossible." But why it is
impossible they never explain.'

Beizer stresses to all whom he meets that his tours are
in no way hostile to the Soviet State. With his scholar's
mind he limits his comments to who lived where, and
when; who was shot where, and why; who petitioned
whom, and to what end. But Beizer is himself a part of
the history he tells. For he is a refusenik, living with his
mother in Leningrad, forced to contemplate an uncertain future. His wife Tatiana and their six-year-old son
Sasha are in Israel, in the southern city of Beersheba. 'I
know so little about them,' Beizer remarks as the tour
comes to an end. 'My son had an accident and lost the

sight of one eye. That is all I know.'

Only the Soviet authorities stand between Misha Beizer and his son. But with the worsening situation of Soviet Jewry, they have added a cruel twist to his hopes of reunion, telling him: 'When your son gets to 21, *he* will decide whether he wants to be a Soviet citizen.'

———◇———

Following Beizer's historical tour, I take a taxi to an address which he has given me. It is on Vasiljevskij Island. Here, in a small apartment, lived Simon Dubnov, the historian of Russian Jewry, murdered by the Nazis in Riga in December 1941. In the same city in which Dubnov once researched and wrote at leisure, Beizer struggles to piece together what he can of facts and details. Dubnov could, and did, travel out of Russia, teach out of Russia, publish and lecture on whatever he wished. Beizer cannot travel, teach or publish. Yet still he works to extend his Leningrad tours, to assemble what information he can about Jewish life in bygone years, and to hope that one day, sooner rather than later, he may be allowed to see his little boy again.

4

At the edge of the pit

Deep snow lies over the city of Minsk, capital of Byelorussia, the White Russian Republic of the Soviet Union. Deep snow lies in and around the pit on Ratomskaya Street, a wide ditch, perhaps fifty yards across, ten yards deep, and a hundred yards long. A few snow-covered trees and bushes dot the edge of the pit. Across the pit, at its far edge, is a wooden fence, and a cluster of low wooden houses.

At the far side, below the fence, is a tall monument, an upright column of stone, inscribed with Russian and Yiddish characters. Outlined in snow, a cluster of wreaths lies at its base. As the inscription reveals, this is a monument to the 8,000 Jews slaughtered at that very spot in 1942, during the Nazi occupation of Minsk. It seems so small a pit, so pathetic a spot, for so large and terrible a disaster.

Standing in front of the monument are two Jews. Both live in Minsk. Both stand proud guard over the tragic memory. Both have also been refused permission to leave the Soviet Union: one for more than three years, the other for more than twelve years. The older man tells of how, on 2 March 1942, at Purim, the Nazis drove more than 8,000 Jews out of the Minsk ghetto to this spot, and machine gunned them. Children were thrown into the pit alive. No one survived.

There were other massacres in and around Minsk: earlier massacres and later ones. Many thousands of Jews had been brought to Minsk at gun-point from surrounding villages. Several thousand had been brought to the city by train from Greater Germany, including Hamburg and Vienna, told by those who deported them that there was work to be done in Minsk, building projects to be completed, agricultural tasks to be performed. No such projects or tasks existed: only the pit here at Ratomskaya Street, and the ditches and ravines of nearby Maly Trostinets.

The older man tells this story without great emotion. He has told it many times before. It was at his insistence that this monument is maintained; that each year it is the focus of one Soviet and two Jewish ceremonies, each remembering the dead. The Jewish ceremonies take place on Purim, the anniversary of the largest of the massacres, and at Tisha B'Av, the anniversary of the destruction of the Temple, a Jewish day of fasting and prayer.

The official Soviet ceremony here at the pit on Ratomskaya Street takes place each year on 9 May, Victory Day. Then, when wartime monuments throughout the Soviet Union are the scene of pilgrimage, speeches, wreath laying ceremonies, this monument is also honoured. The older man has insisted that this should be so. 'Some years ago they didn't allow visits on Victory Day,' he says. 'Nobody came. Just a few Jews. Now they have an official minute of silence. But they no longer allow speeches. They play loud music and don't allow anyone to speak. But they say the ceremonies are loyal.'

The older man tells these things without bitterness, factually, and yet with emphasis. His name is Lev Ovsishcher. Formerly he held the rank of Colonel in the Red Army. In the Second World War he was wounded, and awarded six orders and twelve medals for bravery.

Born on 14 December 1919, in the Vitebsk region of western Russia, Ovsishcher joined the Red Army when he was twenty, as an aviation mechanic. His whole professional life was to be spent in uniform. In 1941 he went to pilots' school, graduating as a pilot, and then becoming a 'Politruk' or political organizer. As a member of the Communist Party, he was then sent on a special Political Commissars' course, becoming, in 1942, a Political Commissar.

That same year, 1942, Ovsishcher was promoted Senior Lieutenant, and sent to the Stalingrad front. There, at the height of the battle, he piloted a plane over the German lines, making in all twenty-four 'propaganda flights', and delivering through a megaphone more than sixty 'broadcasts', including the first Soviet demand for the surrender of von Paulus and his Army. This megaphone 'venture' was later described in the autobiography of a Soviet General. Ovsishcher shows, with pride, the volume itself, *Serving in the Air* by Konstantin Mikhailenko, published in Moscow in 1970.

Later in the battle, Ovsishcher was wounded in the elbow. When the bullet passed through his elbow the sensation was such that he thought his head was 'broken': the bullet had struck a nerve. Dazed, his head spinning, it was some minutes before he realized that the wound was not a fatal one.

The Jews of Hope

On his very next sortie, during a mission to bomb German gun positions, Ovsishcher and his co-pilot crash-landed behind German lines. 'The weather was terrible for the flights,' he recalled. 'The Soviet direction-finding lamp had been destroyed by the German bombardment. So we lost our bearings, and came down on German-controlled territory. We walked towards the nearest village. There, two groups of Germans with dogs were searching for us. All night the Germans searched. It was a dark night, and we walked all night, trying to find our own lines. When it became light, I said I would commit suicide. I did not wish to fall into German hands.'

Ovsishcher and his colleague agreed to commit suicide. 'With the morning light, we lay in a big ditch and prepared to shoot ourselves.' They had sixteen bullets between them, and agreed that each would use his last bullet for himself.

No Germans were near, however, and the two men decided to try once more to find their plane. Their luck held. 'As soon as we saw it, we ran to it. At that moment the Germans also saw us, and ran over to try to shoot us. But we got to the plane and managed to take off while the Germans were still shooting.' Then, airborne and clear of the German fire, they ran out of petrol. Once more they landed in an open field. Fortunately for them, they had crossed back over the Russian lines.

After Stalingrad, Ovsishcher fought on the Kursk front, and later in the battle for Kiev. As the Red Army advanced, he was in White Russia – not far from Minsk itself – and then in Poland. His unit was across the river Vistula from Warsaw when the Warsaw uprising of August 1944 took place. 'Our pilots dropped guns and supplies to Warsaw. I too did it.'

From the Vistula, Ovsishcher continued westward to Berlin. 'I was in Berlin on 8 May 1945.' After the war he went to the Air Force Academy, and in 1950 was promoted Commander. His last posting was as a Staff Officer in the Caucasus, before retiring in 1961 with the rank of Colonel.

How then did Ovsishcher decide to apply for a visa to Israel? By what turn of events and thought did he become, first a conscious Jew, and then a refusenik? His friend, whose name is Boleslav Dobin, listens intently as Ovsishcher tells his tale. 'In my soul I had many talks,' Ovsishcher explains. 'The rising of my national thoughts began amid an anti-Semitic campaign launched in 1953 under the slogan "the struggle against cosmopolitanism". At that time, during the "Doctors' Trial", when many leading Soviet doctors were accused of conspiring to kill the Soviet leaders, the official policy of the State was to show that these doctors were Jews. I began to get interested in Jewish history. I began to understand that we Jews are the people who suffered more than others. I came to understand all the tragedy and all the heroic deeds of our people.'

The anti-Semitic campaign had affected the Air Force Commander personally. 'During the war,' he explains, 'I made about 600 *operational* flights. And then an engineer asked me, "What were *you* doing during the war?" I began to think . . . .'

Ovsishcher's thoughts turned towards Israel. Only three years after the Doctors' Trial, and while the impact of the anti-Semitic campaign was still being felt, Israeli forces defeated the Egyptians in the Sinai campaign of 1956. Even when the State of Israel had been established eight years earlier in 1948, Ovsishcher recalls, 'it was a very happy thought for me. I was pleased when so small a nation protected itself against so many Arabs.'

But neither the Arab-Israel wars of 1948 and 1956, nor the Soviet anti-Semitic campaign of 1953, had led Ovsishcher to think of going to Israel. That thought came in 1967, during the Six-Day War, when the outlook of so many Soviet Jews was transformed. 'In 1967,' Ovsishcher recalls, 'during that wonderful war, I was even more proud, even more happy, and came to the conclusion that the only place for a Jew was Israel. I began to think: "If *we* don't do something for the Jews, who *will* do it?" The return of the Jews to their State is an ongoing process.'

Ovsishcher first applied for a visa to Israel in 1970. His rank and status were an embarrassment to the authorities. 'Many times I was spoken to,' he recalls. In 1972 he was summoned to court with three other senior officers, all living in Minsk, who had applied to go to Israel, among them his friend Colonel Yefim Davidovich. For six months preparations were made for the trial, on a charge of anti-Soviet activity. But then an American Senator intervened, going so far as to tell the Soviet leader, Leonid Brezhnev, that Brezhnev's forthcoming visit to the United States 'would of course go well, but the trial of war veterans in Minsk makes it more difficult'.

The trial was abandoned. But no visas were granted, and Ovsishcher, a war veteran, became, as a result of his application for a visa, an outcast from Soviet society. Within two years he had lost his Colonel's rank, becoming a mere Private, and had been deprived of his

48

At the edge of the pit

Colonel's pension. In 1977 he was interrogated several times in connection with the trial being prepared against Anatoly Shcharansky. In 1979 he was forbidden to leave Minsk, a prohibition that remained in force for several months. Local newspapers derided his request to go to Israel.

Now, after twelve years of waiting in vain for a visa, Ovsishcher looks back over grey years. His daughter Tanya was allowed to leave for Israel in 1978, eight years after her application. But Ovsishcher himself, and his wife Nadezhda, who was not Jewish, were refused permission to follow her. Throughout the Colonel's struggle to leave, it was the support of Nadezhda that sustained him. In January 1983 Nadezhda died. Ovsishcher was alone.

In 1976 Ovsishcher's friend, Colonel Davidovich, one of the war veterans who was to have been tried in 1972, died in Minsk without ever having received permission to leave. More than a thousand Jews and non-Jews attended his funeral, a rare mark of respect. Immediately after Davidovich's death, his wife and daughter were allowed to emigrate to Israel. They were also given permission to take his body to Jerusalem. There, on 27 September 1976, Davidovich was re-buried on the Mount of Olives. I myself was in Jerusalem on that day, and reached the Mount of Olives just as the mourners, many hundreds of Soviet Jews who had been given visas in previous years, were dispersing.

Davidovich and Ovsishcher had both served their country well in the war years. Yet at the time of the outbreak of war in June 1941, Jewish patriotism in the Soviet Union and Jewish loyalty to Communist ideology had been under strain for more than two decades. After

49

brief months of hope at the time of the revolution in 1917, when the Tsarist 'Pale of Settlement' was abolished, there was Jewish rejoicing. A Jewish University was established, and the Jewish disabilities of the Tsarist years ended. But within a few years the new Communist Government had struck swiftly and savagely at Jewish aspirations.

It did so at the very same moment that anti-Communist Russians in the Ukraine, led by a former Tsarist General, Simon Petliura, savagely attacked Jews in hundreds of towns and villages, murdering as many as 80,000 in less than a year. These massacres led to the setting up of many Jewish self-defence groups, and to a mass exodus, both to the United States and to Palestine.

The Ukraine was soon under Communist control. Within a few years Jewish religious activity was being vigorously combated, together with Christian worship; with the upsurge of Jewish interest in a Jewish National Home, Zionism, and the Hebrew language, the main Hebrew-language publishing house was closed down. In 1923 the Jewish Social Democratic Party, the Bund, one of the most active of the pre-war left-wing parties, was declared illegal, and all Jewish self-defence groups disbanded. By 1928 the publication of Hebrew books had been suspended, and many Jewish and Zionist writers imprisoned, or exiled to Central Asia. That same year all Zionist youth groups were declared illegal. Seven years later, in 1935, the principal Communist Jewish newspapers and societies were closed down.

Following the signature of the Nazi-Soviet pact in August 1939, the Soviet Union maintained a steadfast neutrality while Hitler destroyed the independence first of Poland, then of Denmark and Norway, then of

At the edge of the pit

Holland, Belgium and France, and finally of Yugoslavia and Greece. In September 1939 more than 250,000 Polish Jews were able to flee eastwards from Nazi to Soviet rule, to comparative safety, and to survival. But within two months the new border had been closed. Several thousand Jews, living on the Soviet side of the partition line, were arrested and deported to labour camps in northern Russia and Siberia: hundreds perished, but thousands survived.

In June 1941, with the German invasion of the Soviet Union, hundreds of thousands of Jews fought, as did Ovsishcher and Davidovich, in the ranks of the Soviet Army, Navy and Air Force. At the border city of Brest-Litovsk, during the first days of the German onslaught, Chaim Fomin, a Jew, was among the defenders of the city, his heroism recognized in several official Soviet accounts of the battle. At the entrance to the Gulf of Finland, Arseni Arkin, another Jew, was among the heroes of the defence of the Soviet naval base at Hango. In Vilna, Brigadier Jacob Kreiser, also a Jew, was among the leaders of the city's resistance.

Not only on the battlefield, but behind the lines, Jews fought with bravery and tenacity. In Minsk itself, Jewish resistance was continuous through the three years of the German occupation. When, at the approach of Purim in 1942, the Germans demanded that the Jewish Council hand over 5,000 Jews, the Council refused to carry out the order. When it was suggested that the Council should hand over only small children and the elderly, the leaders of the Jewish underground insisted: 'no trading in Jewish souls'.

On the eve of the Purim 'action' by the Germans, it was the Jewish Council members who warned the ghetto

of the impending assault. As a result of this warning
many Jews were able to hide in specially prepared
hiding places, behind cupboards and underneath
floorboards. Even the Commander of the German-
authorized Jewish police urged the Jews of the ghetto to
go into hiding.

The Germans raided the ghetto that Purim, 2 March
1942, driving 8,000 Jews to the Ratomskaya Street pit,
and killing them there. Refusing to be cowed, or broken,
the Jewish Council, while remaining the official link
between the German authorities and the ghetto,
encouraged Jews to escape to the woods. Thousands of
Jews did escape, joining, or forming, partisan groups.
The Jewish Council supplied these groups with clothes,
medicine, food and money. Inside the ghetto, the head of
the Jewish Council, Ilya Moshkin, met the resistance
leaders every Friday afternoon to co-ordinate help.

Moshkin's involvement with the resistance was
discovered by the Germans. He was arrested and
hanged, and all the members of his family murdered.
Another Jew, Joshua Kazinets, who had become the
leader of the entire underground network in Minsk,
Jewish and non-Jewish, was arrested and hanged in the
municipal gardens.

On 28 July 1942 the Germans mounted a second
'action' against the Jews of the Minsk ghetto. On the eve
of the 'action' they ordered the new head of the Jewish
Council, Moshe Yaffe, to address the Jews assembled in
Jubilee Square and to calm them down on the eve of
their execution. Yaffe refused to obey this order. Instead
he shouted to the Jews to run for their lives. The Jews
ran. But more than 25,000 were murdered.

Decimated and starving, the Jews of Minsk continued

to try to escape to the forests. On 16 June 1943 a Jewish doctor, Niuta Jurezkaya, was among those who managed to escape. She was caught, however, and tortured, in the hope that she would reveal something of the resistance movement. 'Who was with you?' she was asked. 'All of my people were with me,' she replied.

Niuta Jurezkaya was shot. Jewish resistance continued in Minsk, as throughout western Russia.

It was in Minsk that a Jew, David Keymakh, organized the assassination of the German ruler of White Russia, Kube, on 22 September 1943. The bomb that killed Kube had been placed in his bedroom by a White Russian maid, E. G. Mazanik. Ironically, on my internal flight from Leningrad to Minsk, the man sitting next to me was reading a newspaper in which Mazanik recalled her deed. But she made no mention of the Jew.

By the end of 1943 Jewish partisans from Minsk had set up six fighting partisan detachments, active in derailing German troop and munition trains, and ambushing German military units. There was also a seventh all-Jewish detachment, known as the Family Detachment, which gave armed protection to more than 600 Jewish women and children hiding in the forests.

Of the 85,000 Jews confined in the Minsk ghetto in the autumn of 1941, as many as 10,000 managed to escape. Half of these survived the war, most of them as partisans.

The Jews in Russia today are proud of their contribution to the war against Nazi Germany. It was a war in which, on Russian soil alone, the Germans massacred more than 1,500,000 Jewish civilians. At Babi Yar, a ravine near Kiev, more than 33,000 Jews were murdered in only three days of September 1941.

The Jews of Hope

Ovsishcher tells me, with the pride of an old soldier, of the Jewish contribution to Russia's struggle for survival during the war years. More than 200 Soviet Jews rose to the rank of General during the war. In one crack unit, the 16th Lithuanian Division, nearly a quarter of the soldiers were Jews. During Ovsishcher's own time as a pilot at Stalingrad, a Jewish General, Israel Baskin, was in command of the artillery on a section of the front. At the southern port of Kerch, a Jewish naval officer, Admiral Paul Trainin, commanded the defence of the naval base. During the Red Army's advance across the Dnieper river in 1943, of 900 soldiers awarded the coveted title of 'Hero of the Soviet Union', twenty-seven were Jews.

In the immediate aftermath of the war, the extent of Jewish suffering, the scale of Jewish participation in the Red Army, and the widespread Jewish partisan activity, all served to revive a sense of Jewish consciousness, of national identity with the Jewish people. In 1948 Golda Meyerson, Israel's first envoy to the Soviet Union, arrived in Moscow. Her visit became the occasion of a massive public gathering, reflecting deep sympathies with and longings for the newly established Jewish State. She herself had been born in Kiev in 1898. As Golda Meir, she was to be Prime Minister of Israel from 1969 to 1974.

The rejoicings at the establishment of the State of Israel were premature, however. Despite the Jewish war record, and Soviet support for the new Jewish State, a series of official anti-Jewish measures, and innumerable anti-Jewish incidents, led to the stamping out of all resurgence of Jewish culture and religious life.

These were the 'black years' of Soviet Jewry, typified,

in 1947, by the arrest of Rabbi Lev of Kharkov who, after refusing to become an informer, was sent to a labour camp, where he died. A year later the actor and producer Salomon Mikhoels, once the director of the Moscow Yiddish Theatre, died after being crushed by a car in Minsk, the very city where I write these notes.

Within days of Mikhoels' death the Yiddish theatre and all Jewish schools were closed, and all linotype machines in the Soviet Union on which Hebrew books used to be printed were smashed. Within a few months, more than 400 leading Jewish writers and scientists were arrested. By 1952 almost all of them had perished in labour camps. Then, on 11 July 1952, twenty-five Jewish intellectuals – one of them a distinguished woman biochemist, Lina Shtern – were brought to trial. A week later all were convicted of the charge of plotting to detach the Crimea from the Soviet Union, in order to turn it into a 'Zionist bourgeois republic' which would serve as 'an American Imperialist base for aggressive anti-Soviet designs'. The twenty-four men were executed on 12 August 1952. Lina Shtern, the only woman, was given a twenty-five-year sentence. Released during the de-Stalinization of the late 1950s, she returned to Moscow, where she died in March 1968, at the age of ninety.

On 13 January 1953 Stalin launched a new attack on Soviet Jewry, accusing a number of Jewish doctors of a widespread and sinister conspiracy against the life of the State. Fourteen doctors were at once arrested and charged with 'sabotage, terrorist and espionage activities'. At the same time, plans were made to deport hundreds of thousands of Jews to Siberia. Stalin's death two months later, before the doctors could be tried or the deportation plans carried out, led to a moment of massive relief among Soviet Jewry. The doctors were released. The deportation plans were shelved. Even Mikhoels was declared to have been an innocent victim. Within five years, however, the Jewish condition again worsened. Jews throughout the Soviet Union were harassed while at prayer, and Jewish shops and houses looted. In Minsk eight Jewish students were arrested for collecting factual material about Israel. Hoping to deter still further any interest in the then ten-year-old Jewish State, *Pravda* described Israel as 'a hell on earth'. Throughout the Soviet Union synagogues were closed down, and in several places the synagogue buildings were confiscated. In the western Soviet town of Chernovtsy several Jews were accused of 'Zionist propaganda' because they had recited the traditional Passover prayer, 'Next Year in Jerusalem'.

During these years 'the Jews of silence' had no choice but to remain silent. To speak as a Jew, or on behalf of Jews, or in a Jewish cause, was dangerous. In July 1961 the first trials began for 'economic crimes', including 'speculation in footwear' and 'speculation in fruit'. The prosecutors demanded the death sentence for 110 people, of whom 68 were Jews. All were shot. In most cases their sentence was given 'without right to appeal', and was immediately followed by the confiscation of their property by the State.

Jews recognized that these sentences had a strong anti-Jewish bias; in Kharkov, for example, in January 1963, all six Jewish defendants were sentenced to death, while the six non-Jewish defendants accused of the same crime received prison sentences. In Leningrad, five Jews were shot; in Moscow, eight; in Chernovtsy, six; in

At the edge of the pit

Kishinev, five and in Minsk, six.

I sit in my hotel room in Minsk, the hotel newly built less than a hundred yards from the Ratomskaya Street pit, and I ponder these facts. I also call to mind having read some years ago the text of a radio broadcast from Minsk on 5 April 1975, on the subject of Judaism. According to this broadcast: 'Judaism is harmful to the Jewish believer because this belief sets him apart from other people, inculcates in him hostility towards other men and makes him oppose the world around him.' These words had cast gloom and fear over the Jews of Minsk. 'Judaism', the broadcaster warned, 'is contrary to our Communist morality, the aims of our society and the progress of modern life.'

———◇———

I walk from my hotel to Lev Ovsishcher's apartment, starting at the Ratomskaya Street pit, past the few surviving houses of the wartime ghetto. The thick snow of the morning has turned into a deep, cold slush. Was it in conditions like this that the victims were driven, half naked, with whips, dogs and guns against them, from the ghetto to the pit? How many cripples, or old people, or tiny children, stumbling over the rough cobbles, were shot down without mercy?

Ovsishcher asks how I reached his apartment, and I reply, 'along the old road from the Ratomskaya Street pit through the former ghetto area'. He tells me that when the Jews of Vienna were brought to Minsk in 1941, believing that they were coming to work, the local Jews said, starkly, 'You are brought here to be killed.' The Jews from Vienna, Ovsishcher recounts, 'became alarmed and excited. The Germans brought up a

57

carriage of water. Everyone was so thirsty they began to drink. After drinking the water they became calm. The water contained a bromide. Shortly afterwards they were killed. No survivors were left. Nobody knows their surnames.'

There is yet another local story of the war years and the deportees. 'There were also Jews brought from Prague. They looked at the local Jews with a sense of being "higher" than the locals. They had been told they would be put in charge here. But all of them were killed . . . .'

At Ovsishcher's apartment two friends arrive, both of them refuseniks like himself. Soviet policy towards Soviet Jews during the 'black years' after the Second World War, which has been so much on my mind, is not their concern, and forms no part of their conversation. They are not dissidents, and they are not seeking to malign the Soviet State. Their one goal is emigration. It is I, the outsider, whose thoughts range over these events of bygone years, especially as they touch on Minsk itself, the city where Mikhoels died . . . .

My thoughts are interrupted by the conversation around me. Ovsishcher is telling his personal story. 'I am in refusal for about twelve years,' he explains. 'At first we were four. My daughter left. Then my mother died, and my wife died. I am the only one left. And now the problem of emigration is to be a kind of zero here. Dobin has been four years in refusal, Sorkin three years. So it is a very tragic situation.'

The 'tragedy' is not only the length of time of refusal, or the closure of emigration. 'Those who hand over their application to emigrate,' Ovsishcher continues, 'are in a terrible position. From the moment I asked for a visa, I lost my military pension and I lost my Colonelcy. I am a simple Private. To be a refusenik is very difficult. Take Dobin here. He can't get a job. There are also very difficult material problems. But for the help of friends, everything would be lost. We three are not alone in this, here in Minsk. There are hundreds of people here who are in such difficulties.'

Since 1970, some 4,000 Jewish families have left the Soviet Union from Minsk, about 10,000 people. Forty thousand Jews are left. They have a synagogue, and those who want to pray can do so. But, says Ovsishcher, 'Jewish culture is in our homes only. Some are lying under the blankets. The only culture allowed is led by the State.'

Despite his appalling personal situation, Ovsishcher talks without despondency, showing with pride photographs of his wife in their younger days. His round, wrinkled face is animated and full of character, of good will. But he chooses his words carefully, and his emphasis is measured, even grave. 'The only thing for which you and our friends in the West must try,' he says, 'is to convince the Soviets to give the full right for those who want to emigrate – to emigrate from here.'

Ovsishcher's wish to emigrate has survived repeated pressures. In 1973 he was interrogated several times by the KGB on threat of a charge of 'anti-Soviet activity'. In 1976 the local newspaper, *Sovietskaya Byelorussia*, accused him of inciting others to anti-Soviet and Zionist activity. He was frequently dismissed from the menial jobs which were all he was allowed, on the grounds that he had a higher education and was taking the place of an unqualified worker.

Twice, in protest against his refusal, Ovsishcher

returned his fifteen medals to the authorities. On the first occasion they were sent back to him. On the second occasion, they were accepted. In May 1979, while walking in Moscow, on his way to synagogue, Ovsishcher was stopped by the KGB, escorted to the airport, and forced to return to Minsk. On 6 July 1979 he was again attacked in *Sovietskaya Byelorussia*, on the grounds that he was not a war hero with fifteen medals.

Ovsishcher's own refusal has been tied up, as so many have been, with his alleged access, in his case many years ago, to military secrets. 'Of course there are some people who had some secrets,' he says. 'But I left the army twenty-two years ago. To this day they are trying to tell me I have some secrets. They are trying to convince *me* it is so.'

Like Evgeni Lein in Leningrad, Ovsishcher does not accept these arguments without challenge. 'I went to the Ministry of Defence in Moscow,' he explains. 'I was told that my refusal was *not* because I had military secrets. I asked them to put it in writing. They said they would not give me any such paper.'

The Ministry of Defence official went on to tell Ovsishcher that they did not believe that the Ministry of Internal Affairs could say his refusal was because of his knowledge of secrets. He went at once to the Ministry of Internal Affairs. But there he was told: 'You are being kept here because of the Ministry of Defence . . .'

Ovsishcher explains how, in yet another effort to break the official refusal to let him go, he had gone to Moscow to see a former army friend, who was both a Colonel and a Jew. This friend was one of the Soviet delegates to an International anti-Fascist Congress, held with Soviet approval. The six Soviet delegates to the Congress, so Ovsishcher's friend reported to him, had handed a petition to the Soviet authorities. All six had signed it, 'to ask the Soviet authorities to let me go'.

The petition had been in vain. But Ovsishcher does not give up. In the typewriter on his desk is yet another, still unfinished, appeal to the authorities. 'I have written *many* letters,' he explains. 'Now I am making a new letter to the Supreme Soviet.'

The former Colonel, now a Private, is emphatic that his wish to leave the Soviet Union, and that of his fellow Jewish refuseniks, is not a provocative or anti-Soviet act. He is not aligning himself with anti-Soviet forces, with enemies of the Soviet Union, or with 'enemies of peace'. He has prepared a statement of his position, which he wishes to be read out at the forthcoming Soviet Jewry Congress in Jerusalem. He makes his statement with the conviction of a man who has never mixed the politics of the day with his single-minded search for an exit visa.

'The Soviet Government', Ovsishcher explains, 'connects the problem of Jewish emigration with peace. They say, "When there will be peace, there will be emigration." There must be détente. At the Congress in Jerusalem the first attention must be put on our wish for peace. That wish for peace must be said loudly. The Congress must respond in favour of peace. All our newspapers say that Israel is an aggressive country. The Jews must therefore raise their voice for peace louder than everyone else.'

In each war, Ovsishcher continues, 'it is the Jews who suffer most. The Congress must make it clear: "We Jews are a peaceful People," and the Jewish love for peace must be stressed everywhere. I am against those steps when my fate is connected with political problems. But if we Jews do not listen to the opinion of the Soviet Union about peace, we shall be out of the play.'

Ovsishcher's friends listen intently as their elder statesman, for such he is to them, goes on to speak of the need for better relations between the Soviet Union and the United States, as an essential prerequisite of renewed Jewish emigration from Russia. 'At the time when Soviet-American relations are becoming sharp,' he says, 'our situation is also becoming sharp. In our souls we are against this link. But we are realists. We must face it.'

Cups of tea, and cakes, are passed round. In this small apartment overlooking Minsk Circus, as darkness falls over the city, it is as if the fate of Soviet Jews can be decided by what Ovsishcher says, by what I pass on. It is as if a visa for Dobin, who waits with his eighty-year-old father, his wife, and his teenage daughter for their refusal to be reversed, will really be granted if the Colonel's words are taken up by world Jewry.

Ovsishcher's dreams, however naïve they may seem to western ears, are sincere, felt with a deep inner force. 'Tell the delegates of the Congress,' he goes on, 'I know very well what war is. I began the war as a military man and ended it as a military man. I know that throughout the war Jewish blood flowed – at the front, in the camps, in the ghettos. I raise my voice *against* war, *against* confrontation.'

Ovsishcher continues: 'There must be made some steps among the nations' leaders to avert a new war. I believe that *then* Jewish emigration will begin again. I want my solid voice against war to be given through you. I again stress, my name must not be used in a political way. As soon as United States-Soviet relations

62

sharpened, the emigration policy became horrible. Of course there were difficult problems in the Second World War between Russia, Britain and the United States. But they *were* able to agree against Fascism. Now, this same point of connection must be found. This will be good for the United States, good for the Soviet Union, *and* good for us, for the Jews. If not, we shall just become like the two sheep who met on a ford across a river. Neither wanted to make way for the other. They were very obstinate. They didn't want to give way – and the tale ends: "Early in the morning two sheep were drowned in this river." Such things can happen with mankind . . . .'

Darkness has fallen. Dobin and Sorkin nod their approval. Is it really possible for words to move mountains? Ovsishcher, who forty years earlier had been witness to the worst of mankind's cruelties, knows in his heart that all must not be lost. His wife has died. His daughter has gone. But the world situation seems to him to be the ultimate barrier to Jewish hopes. 'When everyone in the Soviet Union says so much about the struggle for peace,' he says, 'I am convinced that no one needs peace in the world as much as Jews do. Israel is fighting and losing so much blood, not because she wants war, but because she wants to survive. But our voice for peace might be heard. At each forum and at each Congress we must be the voice for peace.'

I write down Ovsishcher's words, as he expresses them, content to be his mouthpiece. When he has finished, I think to myself: 'How foolish the Soviet authorities are, not to allow this man to go, to give his message himself in Jerusalem.' It is not given to me, however, to understand the workings of Soviet official-dom: of the minds of the same men who, seven years earlier, allowed Ovsishcher's friend and fellow soldier, Colonel Davidovich to go to Jerusalem, but only in a coffin.

Does Ovsishcher himself really believe that he will ever be given a visa? I dare not ask him this question, but he answers it nevertheless. 'We have not lost hope', he says, 'that our time will come. We are Jews. We do not lose hope. We are waiting for our hour.'

In Minsk, the refusenik struggle has been much affected by the death of Ovsishcher's wife. A non-Jewish woman, Nadezhda Ovsishcher had brought much strength and courage to the movement in that city. The Jewish festival of Simchat Torah – the Rejoicing of the Law – had been celebrated in a muted way that year, such had been the impact of her death.

But now Ovsishcher has regained his strength, and looks to the outside world to help the cause of Soviet Jewry. His final words are for the outside world, for the concerned Jews and non-Jews in the West, for the campaigners for Soviet Jewry: 'Tell our friends at the Congress', he says, ' "thank you for not forgetting us. Such things help us to guard our strength. Thanks to you, we do not lose hope." '

———◇———

The first meeting is always with strangers. The second meeting is with friends. In their isolation, and in the trap of their 'refusal', these Jews need visitors from the West, and respond immediately to them, drawing the visitor into the warmth of their homes and the intimacy of their aspirations.

Returning to Ovsishcher's apartment the next day, I find Dobin and Sorkin already there. We renew our conversation, but we do so now as old friends. Photographs are produced, family stories exchanged, some special biscuits have already been set on the table. But it is the problem of Jewish emigration which is still uppermost in all minds: host, guests and visitors. Ovsishcher, who was born in the same Russian province as the painter, Marc Chagall, remarks: 'I hope that if I can leave in the near future, I will meet Chagall in Paris – and invite him to visit me in Israel, as my guest.'

Ovsishcher now ponders a way forward based on a western initiative. The western countries, he suggests, must propose to the Soviet Union to prove their belief in peace 'by steps leading to a renewal of Jewish emigration'. Once more, Ovsishcher wishes me to pass on a message. 'You must make it clear', he says, 'that one of the steps to prove the Soviet belief in peace would be the release of Jews. That should be made clear, at Madrid, at Geneva, at Jerusalem . . . .'

Today, as yesterday, Dobin and Sorkin have listened attentively to Ovsishcher's words. Over the years, they, like so many Jews in Minsk, have gained courage from his strength. Dobin is middle-aged, and silent. His four years as a refusenik have not been easy for him. The rules and regulations, the need to re-apply every six months, the difficulty with documents, the changing excuses for refusal, all have been used as a trap against these people, to keep them in, first when tens of thousands were allowed to go each year, and now, when emigration has all but halted. 'It would be amusing', Dobin comments, 'if it were not so tragic.'

Sorkin, who is in his early thirties, had taken his emigration papers to the Visa Office, only to be told that they would not even agree to receive them. 'Why?' he asked. 'Because your mother does not want to go.' This refusal even to process applications is becoming more frequent, not only in Minsk. Even to reach the 'status' of refusenik is now a struggle, and for an increasing number, impossible.

Sorkin speaks of the past. Of how his grandfather Alexander Sorkin had been killed by the Nazis during the first days of the war, during the first random killings of Jews in Minsk. Sorkin, born eleven years later, was named after him. Now a refusenik, the young Alexander is compiling a collection of Yiddish songs. He is helped in this task by another young Jew, not a refusenik, who has put together quite a large number of songs, which they sing at Jewish weddings. Sorkin is the guitarist. But this can only be done privately. When, on 20 December 1977, the young Jews of Minsk approached the authorities for permission to establish a Jewish folk dance and song group, 'and to do it loyally', as Sorkin explained, the authorities warned them not to proceed. 'Jewish culture', Sorkin comments, 'has to be done from under a blanket.'

Another young man enters Ovsishcher's apartment. He will be thirty years old in two months' time. By trade he is a driver, a working man. His desire to live as a Jew in Israel reflects the simplicity of the cause, and its single-mindedness. In 1976 he applied to go to Israel. Since then he has not even been allowed to continue his simple profession. Now he is a house painter. Many of his relatives were killed in the Minsk ghetto during the war. In 1979 his parents were given their visas, and now live in Israel. But still he is not allowed to go. Since he first applied, he has had two sons. Sometimes with friends, but mostly by himself, he is learning Hebrew.

At the edge of the pit

The young man, Gennady Feldman, grew up in a Yiddish-speaking family. 'There was a kind of Jewish atmosphere,' he recalls, but he did not even think about going to synagogue, or to Israel. In 1973 he was serving in the Soviet Army as a driver. It was at the time of the October War, when Egypt and Syria had attacked Israel on the Day of Atonement, the most solemn day in the Jewish calendar. The Soviet press was vitriolic in its denunciation of Israel, which was portrayed, in articles and cartoons, as a Fascist power. In the young man's unit there was an organized discussion of one of those newspaper articles. 'I was the only Jew in a group of a hundred soldiers. I saw that they looked at me because I was the only Jew. At that time I didn't think of going to Israel. But after that, after the army, I began to get in touch with Jews. I went to synagogue. There is an age in a person when he begins to grow, when my national understanding began to grow. I thought, "Now it is my time to go." '

The young man is silent for a moment. Then he adds: 'Even those Jews who don't want to go now, at the end point, they will go.'

It is time to leave, this second visit over, and to take the night train back to Moscow. As we say goodbye in his doorway, Ovsishcher speaks to me for the last time. 'When the talk about us begins,' he says, 'you must say to the Soviet authorities, "When you speak of your belief in human values, why are you holding people here? Why don't you let them go?" ' Then, with a desperate sadness in his voice, his eyes suddenly weak, he adds: 'I have my only daughter in the West. I want to be re-united with my daughter.'

5

From Rumbuli to Jerusalem

---◇---

The Rumbuli forest lies outside Riga, twenty minutes from the city by bus, near the airport. In 1941 and 1942 it was the site of the mass execution of tens of thousands of Riga Jews, and of more than 20,000 Jews brought to Riga from the cities and towns of Germany.

Twenty years after these massacres, Rumbuli was a deserted site, marked by no memorial. The Jews of Riga shunned it. But with the re-awakening of Jewish consciousness in the Soviet Union in the 1960s, Rumbuli, like other mass murder sites, including Babi Yar in Kiev and the Ratomskaya Street ravine in Minsk, became a focal point of the Jewish renaissance.

Among those who went out to Rumbuli in those years was a fourteen-year-old schoolgirl, Ruth Alexandrovich. Twenty years later, sitting in the soothing sun of a Jerusalem afternoon, she recalls those visits to the sombre site. 'Twice a year we went there. It was an empty place. A few of us came to clean it, to cover the bones.'

Eventually, the Soviet authorities gave permission for the Jews to put up a memorial stone on the Rumbuli site. The words on the stone were inscribed in both Russian and Yiddish. But they were not allowed to make any specific reference to 'Jews', only to 'victims'.

Once the memorial was set up, more and more Riga Jews went out to Rumbuli, to care for the site, and to tend it. Sometimes Jewish memorial meetings were held there. At other times the Soviet authorities sent a speaker or a singer to conduct a memorial service. 'But nobody spoke the word Jew.'

The Jews of Riga continued to flock to Rumbuli on days of remembrance. 'Our Zionism was born there,' Ruth Alexandrovich recalls. 'For Riga's Jewish youth it was a place where they recognized their Judaism. I was fourteen when I recognized I was a Jew.'

In 1965 the Jews of Riga had spent only twenty years under Soviet rule. Before that, before the four years of Nazi torment, the city had been the capital of independent Latvia. Only grandparents could recall the years before the First World War, when Riga had been a part of the Tsarist Empire, as well as a centre of Jewish emigration to western Europe and the United States. Among those born in Riga was Isaiah Berlin, the British philosopher, and one time President of the British Academy. Among those who perished in Riga was the historian Simon Dubnov, murdered by the Nazis at the age of eighty-one.

The Jews of Riga who gathered at Rumbuli in the 1960s did not confine their awakening to Jewish history, culture or language. Many began to apply to go to Israel. It was a time when the Soviet Union still had diplomatic relations with Israel: when an Israeli Ambassador resided in Moscow, and was able to travel to many Jewish communities: when visiting Israeli delegations and sportsmen were the focal point of Jewish identity and enthusiasm.

In December 1966 Ruth Alexandrovich, then aged nineteen, applied with her parents for an exit visa. Six months later, following the Six-Day War, the Soviet Union broke off diplomatic relations with Israel. The applications had been in vain.

———◇———

For the Jews of Kiev, it was the ravine of Babi Yar that became a focal point of identity with Jewishness. There, in a shallow, sandy valley, more than 33,000 Jews were massacred in September 1941. In memory of that massacre, an official Soviet memorial meeting was held on 29 September 1968. Hundreds of Jews attended, but, to their horror, heard the official speakers denounce, not the Nazi killings, but Israel. A Jew, Boris Kochubievsky, overheard two Soviet citizens talking thus:

Man: 'What's going on here?'
Woman: 'Here the Germans killed a hundred thousand Jews.'
Man: 'That wasn't enough.'

Boris Kochubievsky exploded with rage, protesting to the authorities. Two months later, on 28 November 1968, he was given permission to emigrate to Israel. But nine days later he was arrested. At his trial, which began on 13 May 1969, his brother was prevented from entering the court by a 'cordon' of citizens. 'But I am Kochubievsky's brother,' he protested. 'You're not a brother,' one of the cordon organizers replied. 'You're a Yid, a Yid, a Yid.'

On 16 May 1969 Kochubievsky was sentenced to

three years in a 'severe regime' labour camp. As he left the court he expressed his hope 'that no one else will share my lot because of his desire to go to Israel.' Having served his term, Kochubievsky was allowed to go to Israel. But many others were to be forced to share his 'lot' – arrest, trial and imprisonment – as the desire to go to Israel became more and more widespread.

In the late 1960s many young Jews began to learn Hebrew, and to teach it. In Moscow, in October 1969, during the Jewish festival of Simchat Torah – the Rejoicing of the Law – thousands of young Jews filled the quarter-mile length of Arkhipov Street, on either side of the Central Synagogue, singing and dancing through a cold drizzle until late in the night. Observers were staggered by their knowledge of Hebrew and Yiddish songs: songs never taught in Soviet schools, and not openly sung for more than forty years. Some of those present, many of them youngsters, held pieces of paper on which they had written all the Hebrew words they had been able to collect.

The desire to learn modern Hebrew had become a symbol of Jewish national identity. It was indeed a Russian Jew, Eliezer Ben Yehuda, who, ninety years earlier, had gone to Jerusalem specifically to turn biblical Hebrew into the language of the new Jewish commonwealth: a modern language for the daily life of a modern nation.

Among the teachers of Hebrew in Leningrad who sought in the 1960s to revive the Hebrew language, and to use it as a base for eventual emigration, was Gilya Butman. In 1969 he was thirty-seven years old. His grandfather, lost without trace in the Second World War, had been found, alive, in a kibbutz in Israel. He sent Gilya an invitation. Gilya applied for emigration, but his application was turned down.

In June 1970 Butman was among several hundred Leningrad Jews who protested in public against the Soviet Government's refusal to grant them permission to leave. He was also aware of a dangerous enterprise which had its origins among a small group of Jews, mostly from Riga. Their plan was to seize a twelve-seater Soviet civilian aeroplane, fly it across the Soviet border with Finland, land in Sweden, and then, allowing the aeroplane to be returned to the Soviet Union, make their way to Israel.

On 15 June 1970, the day the escape was to take place, all those directly involved were seized by the militia. Six months later, the twelve leaders were tried in the Leningrad City Court, and sentenced to long terms in 'strict regime' labour camps. Two of the would-be hijackers, Mark Dymshits and Edouard Kuznetsov, were sentenced to death.

On 25 December 1970, as the sentences were announced in the Leningrad courtroom, cheers of approval broke out from the specially invited citizen-audience. But these cheers were silenced by the shouts of the relatives of the accused. 'Good fellows!', 'Hold on!', they called out, from another part of the courtroom. 'We are with you! We are waiting for you! We shall be in Israel together!'

Following widespread western protests, the two death sentences were commuted to fifteen years' imprisonment. The convicted men, nine Jews and two non-Jews, were sent to prison and labour camp. They became known in the West as 'Prisoners of Zion'. Campaigns were launched to release them. But only after ten years, when most of their sentences were due to expire, were all but three of them released. Those released were allowed to go to Israel. The two non-Jews, Yury Fedorov and Aleksei Murzhenko, remained prisoners, despite the continued efforts of many Jewish campaigners in the West to have them released. Yosif Mendelevich, the last of the Jews to be held, was released in February 1981, almost eleven years after being sentenced.

The severity of the Leningrad sentences did not deter those who were now determined to try to emigrate. On 26 February 1971 twenty-four Riga Jews marched to the Visa Office to demand the right to leave. Two days later, thirty Moscow Jews staged a 'sit-in' at the Supreme Soviet building, in protest against their 'refusal'. But these courageous gestures were overshadowed, within a few weeks, by a second 'show' trial.

This second trial was also held in Leningrad. There were nine defendants, including Gilya Butman, Hebrew teacher and friend of the first Leningrad prisoners. In a statement to the court, Butman declared that the instances of anti-Semitism which he had experienced in the Soviet Union, together with his own studies of Jewish history and the Hebrew language, had brought him 'to the thought of Israel, and the need to struggle to keep Soviet Jews a nation'. It was in that context that he had helped the would-be hijackers.

On 20 May 1971 Butman was sentenced to ten years in prison. He too served his term, far beyond the various remission dates, despite many western protests on his behalf. After his release in May 1979, he was allowed to go to Israel. There, twelve years after he had received his sentence, I sat with him in a Jerusalem restaurant and walked with him in the Jerusalem sun. He had survived a decade of incarceration not only with unbroken spirit, but with his faith in Jewish statehood unimpaired.

The second Leningrad trial was not to be the last that year. Only four days after Butman and the other eight defendants had been sentenced, a further trial took place in Riga. There were four defendants. One of them was Ruth Alexandrovich, the Riga schoolgirl whose sense of Jewish identity had first been stirred at Rumbuli. In 1966 she and two of her girl friends had been expelled from the Young Communist League for having submitted requests to emigrate. She had been a member of the League for four years. Now she was twenty-three years old, and a nurse.

In May 1969 Ruth Alexandrovich had become involved in operation 'Pushkin', a plan to collect and distribute leaflets on Jewish history. There were three leaflets in all, entitled 'Home', 'For the Return of Soviet Jews to their Homeland', and 'Your Native Tongue'. Ruth had passed on the first leaflet to someone else, to be duplicated. She had herself duplicated six copies of the second leaflet, in August 1969; and in December 1969 she had duplicated fifteen copies of 'Your Native Tongue'.

During the course of her cross-examination, Ruth defended the three leaflets, telling the court: 'In the Soviet newspapers they write with bias against Israel. In the Soviet Union there are no Jewish schools.' Hence her own involvement in helping to distribute these materials.

At the end of the trial Ruth was invited to make a final statement. 'I admit the facts contained in the charge,' she told the court, 'but I never pursued the aims of undermining and weakening the Soviet regime. My aim is the self-determination of the Jewish nation, and in this sense I am a Zionist. The spirit of socialist ideas is close to me and I see no contradiction in this with my desire to go to Israel.'

Ruth ended: 'I rely on the just decision of the court.' But the court was determined to deter the spread of Jewish knowledge, of what Ruth had described to the court as her 'national awareness'. She was sentenced to one year's deprivation of freedom, in prison and in labour camp: the first Jewish woman to be incarcerated in this way since the Stalin era. She too became a 'Prisoner of Zion'. For six months she was in Riga prison. While she was in prison, her parents were allowed to leave for Israel. At the same time, international pressure mounted for her to be allowed to go to Israel once her sentence was over.

After six months in prison, Ruth was sent to Potma labour camp. There she remained for the last six months of her sentence. Then she was released, and told that she could leave the Soviet Union. 'I had no passport for foreign travel. They gave me a paper, and said "go". Three weeks later, I left.'

Ruth Alexandrovich was the first 'Prisoner of Zion' to reach Israel. Twelve years later, her days as a refusenik, as a prisoner, and as a Soviet Jew far behind her, she tells me her story in the shade of a Jerusalem balcony. But now, so long after her own struggle had ended in emigration, the struggle of others is no less vivid for her. Ruth Alexandrovich fears, as do so many of those who have been allowed to leave, that the plight of Soviet Jewry, and of the refuseniks, has 'returned to its worst days'.

'I know so much about the problem,' Ruth reflects.

The Jews of Hope

'But I don't have the prescription – what to do to help them. It hurts.'

———◇———

In 1969, a year before the first Leningrad trial, 3,000 Jews had been allowed to leave the Soviet Union. In 1970 the number had fallen to just over 1,000. And then, within a year of the two Leningrad trials, and the Riga trial, the gates of emigration had opened. By 1972 the first 13,022 Jews of the eventual half a million who were to leave in the next decade, had left for abroad. It is those gates that closed in 1982, trapping so many tens of thousands behind them. The decade of mass emigration was over.

Between 1968 and 1981 a total of 641,336 Soviet Jews asked for invitations to Israel; these invitations being the basic document demanded by the Soviet authorities in order to process an application. All 641,336 invitations were in fact sent. But up to the end of 1981 only 259,635 permissions to emigrate had been granted. This leaves more than 380,000 Soviet Jews who had wanted to leave sufficiently to have asked for an invitation, but who have so far been unable to gather the many documents needed before they can begin to process their application. A few of these, after receiving the invitations, may have decided not to use them. A few died before their invitations reached them. But there are still more Jews inside the Soviet Union who have requested invitations than there are Soviet Jews who have been given a visa.

Since 1980 the Soviet authorities have increased significantly the barriers to making an application. As each Jew whom I met reiterated, the basic document, needed before any of the others can be of use, is the formal invitation, or *vyzov*, from a relative in Israel. For the ten years of mass emigration, this term 'relative' was widely interpreted. But in recent years many thousands of requests for emigration have not even been accepted for processing by the Visa Office, on the grounds that the 'family kinship is insufficient'. Only invitations from parents, or from children, will be accepted for an application.

This severe restriction was first introduced in Odessa early in 1980. Subsequently it was applied in most of the cities in the Ukraine. By the end of 1982 it had been introduced in almost every Soviet Republic. As a result of this restriction, a new category of Soviet Jew has come into existence, one who neither received his exit visa, nor had his visa application 'refused', but who is deprived of the opportunity even of submitting an application.

Two further restrictions added difficulties even for those who did receive invitations from their parents or their children. First, the working hours of many Visa Offices were curtailed, and the Offices themselves closed on certain days of the week, as happened in Baku, Kishinev, Chernovtsy, Odessa and Minsk. Then, invitations which were known to have been sent from close relatives in Israel, and sent by registered post, were not delivered to the addressee by the Soviet postal authorities.

Another barrier to emigration was introduced in 1982. Until then, the invitation, once it had been submitted with a visa application, could be renewed in the event of a further application being needed. In 1982 refuseniks were suddenly told that they would need an entirely new invitation. First in Moscow, then elsewhere, even an unprocessed invitation ceased to be valid after six months.

In 1982 the granting of the visas themselves was drastically curtailed. Nor did the pattern for 1983 show any change, except in the direction of further restrictions. This in itself inhibits people from asking for invitations. In March 1983 a total of 101 visas were issued. This was a half of the total in March 1982, a twelfth of those granted in March 1981, a thirtieth of those for March 1980, and less than a fortieth of the visas issued in March 1979. Only one of the March 1983 visas went to someone from Moscow, and not a single visa was issued to any of the 10,000 refuseniks.

These 10,000 refuseniks are without a doubt those most highly motivated of all Soviet Jews to leave the Soviet Union, and to go to Israel. They are the ones who seek to learn Hebrew, to study Jewish history, and, for a growing number, to practise Judaism, despite the constant pressures to desist from such activities. But at present they have little hope of a visa: some would say, no hope at all. Among those who still wait, and hope, are Benyamin Bogomolny and his wife Tanya. Born on 7 April 1946, Benyamin first applied for an exit visa when he was twenty. Now he is thirty-seven. To his amazement, someone sent him the *Guinness Book of World Records* for 1982, in which he appears, on page 388, as 'the most patient refusenik'. His wife writes from Moscow, where they live: 'The news about these precious couple of lines has spread about, and many people here believe that it may help us.' Surely, she goes on to ask, 'this is the kind of record no country would wish to keep for a long time!'

Forced to remain 'in refusal', driven out of their professions, castigated for wanting to go to Israel, the

1   Evgeni Lein in court (see pages 8–16). This photograph was surreptitiously taken by a refusenik through the courtroom door.

 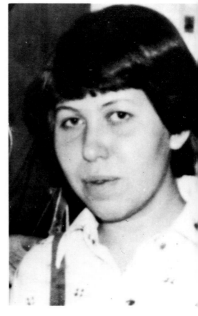

2 *top* Prayers outside the courthouse during Lein's trial (page 10).

3 *left* Evgeni Lein.

4 *right* Nehama Lein.

5 Mikhail (Misha) Beizer during one of his Leningrad tours (pages 32–42).

6 *top* Police Bridge, Leningrad, scene of an attempted assassination in 1903 (page 38).

7 *bottom* Mikhail (Misha) Beizer and the author (page 39), in front of the former Cheka (Secret Police) building in Leningrad.

8 *above* The word *Evrei* (Jew) as it appears in the 'nationality' section of a Soviet identity card (known as the passport).

9 *below* A Soviet cartoon of 1981: Jew and Nazi are yoked together and seeking to enslave the Ukraine.

10 *above* Yuly Kosharovsky (pages 92–109) in a Moscow street.

11 *below* Eli Kosharovsky with his father: a photograph taken in his father's study.

12 Yuly Kosharovsky in Moscow in March 1983. An inadvertent double exposure, this photograph was released by the Soviet authorities who mistook it for the Henley regatta which forms the background (see also photograph 18).

13 Colonel Ovsishcher in Minsk, after the emigration of his daughter and the death of his wife: he is holding a photograph of himself and his wife in earlier days.

refuseniks feel all the more strongly that their true home is in the Jewish State. But this sense of nationhood is not new for Soviet Jews or for their Russian forebears. A hundred years ago it was seen in the pioneering efforts of Russian Jews in Palestine, establishing farms and villages, draining swamps, setting up schools, making Hebrew the language of daily life. In the 1920s Jews from Russia were among the founders of the political structure, and of the idealistic base of the Jewish National Home. The first four Prime Ministers of the State of Israel were all born on Russian soil: Ben Gurion in one of the Polish provinces of the Pale of Settlement, Moshe Sharett in the Black Sea port of Kherson, Levi Eshkol and Golda Meir in the Ukraine. The first four Presidents, Chaim Weizmann, Yitzhak Ben-Zvi, Zalman Shazar and Efraim Katzir, were likewise Russian-born. Menachem Begin, who became Prime Minister of Israel in 1977, was born a subject of the Russian Tsar, four years before the fall of the Tsarist Empire.

Today's Soviet refuseniks seek only to be able to contribute to the evolution of Israel's life, as their fellow Russian Jews have done throughout the past century. Those who had left Russia for Palestine had been few in number, but they brought determination and vision with them. Between 1905 and 1914, the years in which more than a million Jews emigrated to the United States, 24,000 made the journey from Russia to Palestine. In 1909 it was primarily Russian-born Jews who founded the town of Tel Aviv on the sand dunes north of Jaffa. Meir Dizengoff, under whose guidance Tel Aviv became a modern city, had been born in Russia, and had been active in the Russian revolutionary movement in the 1880s. Arrested as a revolutionary in 1885, he first went to Palestine in 1892, to establish a glass factory.

It was also in Russia that Mendel Beilis was accused, in Kiev, of ritual murder – the revived medieval 'blood libel' – alleging that Jews used Christian blood to bake their Passover bread. Beilis was brought to trial championed in the West, properly defended in court, and found not guilty. In 1914 he reached Palestine. Later he recalled in his memoirs how 'the Land of Israel had an invigorating effect upon me; it gave me new life and hope.'

Between the wars, Jews continued to reach Palestine from Ukrainian pogroms and Soviet oppression. They too helped to lay the foundations of Jewish statehood. Not for them the Stalinist counterpart, the Jewish Autonomous Region of Birobidjan, set up in 1934 to be Communism's answer to the Land of Israel. By 1941 there were only 30,000 Jews in the Region, a tenth of Stalin's target. By 1959 Nikita Krushchev admitted that the scheme had failed, blaming the failure on 'Jewish individualism'. By 1976 there were less than 12,000 Jews in the Region, forming only a fifteenth of the total population. Less than one in five of those Jews spoke Yiddish, despite a Yiddish daily newspaper. Recently, a Yiddish grammar was published there. But the Hebrew language, having no place in the Soviet view of a Jewish Region, was neither taught nor spoken.

The vibrant Jewish life of pre-revolutionary Russia did not die a natural death. It was broken up, suppressed, distorted and forced into silence over a period of more than five decades. But it was not destroyed in its entirety. During the decade of mass emigration, a renewed Jewish consciousness emerged, which even today's 'nil' emigration cannot crush.

6

'We just want to buy a ticket . . . .'

———◇———

Throughout Moscow and Leningrad, and to a smaller extent in Kiev, Minsk, Riga and Kharkov, small groups of dedicated Jews meet in private apartments to study Hebrew. Each lesson usually takes place once a week, and lasts for two to four hours. These are no ordinary gatherings. The authorities continuously break up such classes, take the names of those present, seek to prevent the class from gathering again, interrogate pupils at the police station and threaten to throw them out of their university or professional work.

The refuseniks, however, and those other Jews who wish to prepare themselves for the possibility of emigration, however remote, do not allow this pressure to deter them. Day by day, in different parts of the cities, tucked away amid the vast apartment blocks of Soviet suburbia, Jews sit at a kitchen table, or in a small study, learning Hebrew, the language of the Bible and of modern Israel.

Cut off from access to most Hebrew books, their mail often intercepted, their chance of study hampered by the lack of material, these students of all ages – young people of university age, adults and old age pensioners, peer at the blackboards and slide-screens upon which the alphabet, grammar and literature of the Hebrew language are presented, and listen to tapes of stories and exercises. There are no youngsters in these classes. It is a criminal offence under Soviet Law to teach 'religion' to anyone under sixteen, and teaching Hebrew can, if the authorities choose, come under the category of 'religion'.

The progress of many of the pupils is amazing. Often, after only a year's study, a pupil can converse in fluent Hebrew. Some of the veteran Hebrew teachers write Hebrew poetry and prose in language which is on a par with literary works written in Israel by Israelis.

Hebrew teachers in Moscow and Leningrad ensure that Hebrew teaching goes on, despite the continual pressure against it. Their pupils can only meet privately, in groups of five or six, or even singly. Even so, it is estimated that, in these two cities alone, the number of Jews actually engaged in learning Hebrew is in the thousands. Many, once they have mastered it, will teach it in their turn.

As the work of each group advances, its members begin to converse in Hebrew alone. Although teaching and studying Hebrew is legally permitted, by Soviet Law, these groups are denied access to the teaching materials they would like to use. Often the books are tattered, the slides worn, the tapes indistinct. But the lessons have a keenness which keeps the visitor enthralled. 'Three pupils, joined by a fourth,' I noted in my diary as a Hebrew lesson materialized around me late one Moscow afternoon. 'The teacher is full of zeal and humour.'

Copies had been made of a four-month-old issue of a beginner's newspaper, published in Jerusalem, and given to each pupil at the end of last week's lesson. All four had been asked to read it, and to give this week a 'report' on it, in Hebrew. Amid much laughter, the reports are made, followed by a discussion, also in Hebrew, of recent Israeli controversies.

Visitors are often surprised by the humour and light-heartedness of these small groups, meeting amid such adversity, and trapped in a land they wish to leave. Laughter, and a total lack of self-pity, are the hallmarks of so many of these gatherings. But the fears are always there: fears that last year's 'refusal' will be permanent, that the rate of emigration will never return to its earlier heights, that a son will be called up for military service and be told: 'now that you have had access to military secrets, you cannot go', that a friend will be imprisoned or exiled to serve as a warning to others, or that the international interest and pressure, seen by the refuse-niks as so vital to their prospects, will decline.

The present 'nil' level of emigration, I was told, is a part of a systematic effort by the authorities to try to crush the morale of the movement: to say to those who are thinking of embarking upon the emigration process, itself so difficult and fraught with danger, 'why begin?', 'why risk your job?', 'why risk the hostility of your neighbours?', 'why cast a cloud over your children's education?', 'why become an "outcast" of society?', 'why start the Hebrew classes and other cultural activities which are *against* the society here, and thus risk, if you become too active, the fate of . . . ?'

Every Russian Jew knows the fate of Anatoly Shcharansky, sentenced in July 1978 – at the age of thirty – to thirteen years' 'deprivation of liberty' for having been at the centre of the fight for visas and for human rights. A refusenik since 1973, refused permission since 1974 to follow his wife Avital to Jerusalem, Shcharansky demanded the right of emigration for all Soviet Jews with courage, zeal and humour.

From the moment that the Soviet Union signed, in 1975, the Helsinki Agreement, giving every individual the right 'to leave any country, including his own', Shcharansky was active in an unofficial group set up in Moscow to monitor Soviet observance of the agreement for Jew and non-Jew alike. Three weeks before his trial, his friend Vladimir Slepak, the other Jewish member of the Helsinki monitoring group, was sentenced to five years' exile in Siberia, while on the same day as Slepak's trial and sentence another leading refusenik, Ida Nudel, herself the friend of the existing 'Prisoners of Zion', received a four year sentence.

The sentencing of Slepak, Nudel, and above all of Shcharansky, was a severe blow, and had been intended as a severe blow, to all Soviet Jews who were already 'in refusal', or who contemplated emigration. Yet, as Shcharansky was driven away from the Moscow courtroom after his sentence, the many Jews gathered outside sang with fervour the Zionist and Israeli national anthem, *Hatikvah*, 'Hope'.

Every Russian Jew knows the threat that hovers over him once he seeks to leave; is familiar with the terrible fate of those sixteen or more activists who are in prison or in exile; knows of the risks that a refusenik runs of an ever-increasing circle of pressure and punishment. And yet, I was told, the authorities avoid making 'the last irrevocable step', hesitate to impose even stricter penalties and more savage punishments.

Perhaps, one refusenik told me, the authorities realize

that they can never really crush 'the Jewish heart which always hopes'.

In place of visas, debates. In place of the right to leave, discussions. In place of the free movement of peoples across borders, hopes and plans for the future. This process of debating, discussing, planning is itself a lifeline. But it is shadowed now by considerable fears, following the current clamping down on emigration to Israel. 'It is not a closure of emigration,' one refusenik asserts, 'but putting a question about this closure. It is a challenge by the authorities, made in a menacing way. If this challenge is not answered as energetically as it is made, the most pessimistic forecasts may come true.'

Darkness has fallen. Walking in the snow, a group of refuseniks discuss the question of 'nil' emigration: 'What is to be done?' Lenin's question of sixty years ago, is their question now. As they rehearse the facts, figures, past prospects, present impasse, they see, as one very real barrier to renewed emigration, the fact that the majority of Soviet Jews who were given visas after 1977 went, not to Israel but to the United States. The Soviet authorities gave each of these emigrants an exit visa to leave for Israel, and only for Israel.

One of those present at this debate asks, 'How can the Soviet authorities allow America to be the destination of so many tens of thousands, without rousing expectations among millions of other Soviet citizens that they too might try to go to the United States?'

Whether this is actually an argument used in the Kremlin, none of the speakers knows. They are denied the possibility of an open debate, of a real discussion with the authorities. They therefore rehearse every possibility, probe every theory: and so the 'destination' debate goes on.

On a material level, Israel cannot compete with the inducements offered by what has for a hundred years been the 'Golden Land' of Russian Jewish lore and dreams. But, if, instead of flights to Vienna, there were only direct flights to Israel, then, so one refusenik argues, the Soviet authorities would be able to say to any non-Jewish applicant: 'Look, it is to Israel, and to Israel alone.' At the same time, so another refusenik suggests, let the Jew who had intended to go to America from the very start of his application at least *see* Israel, glimpse its landscape, meet its people, and, who knows, he may actually *want* to stay. The distaste for going to Israel is, after all, in large part a result of Soviet anti-Israel propaganda, paraded almost daily in the Soviet press.

Do not forget, I am told, that for the last sixty years there has been, for the Jews of Russia, cultural assimilation and an erosion of Jewish national feeling as a result of an uninterrupted, single-minded, secular, Communist education. At the same time, many of the Jews who leave are either the children of mixed marriages, or are themselves married to non-Jews; their sense of Jewish identity is minimal. Remember also the Soviet policy of isolating Soviet Jews both from Israel and from world Jewry, by the jamming of Israeli broadcasts, and the persistent interference with postal and telephonic communication overseas. Since July 1982 the Soviet authorities have also closed all direct-dialling facilities between the Soviet Union and the outside world.

Two further factors increased the movement of Soviet Jews to the United States between 1975 and 1980: the ability of Jews, or anyone, once in the West, to choose where they wished to go, and the growing number of close relatives in the United States towards whom the later emigrants were understandably drawn.

The debate evolves. Let the Soviets be assured that Tel Aviv and not New York is the initial destination of all Jews who leave. Let the individual Jew then decide, freely, where he wants to go. After all, once in the West, he acquires the freedom to take aeroplanes and to cross borders at will, so he can go where he pleases, when he pleases. But let him make that choice only when he has reached, and seen, the land for which, alone, his visa was granted.

One of the debaters comments, earnestly, as the snow flurries thicken into a dense grey gloom: 'A Jew applies to go to Israel. It is the only place he can apply to, in order to have his application considered. His application is granted, and he *does* go there, physically. Let him go where he likes *once* he has reached Israel. But let him do it on his own cost. Let him buy a ticket with his own money.'

'With his own money?' asks another. 'Yes,' replies the first, 'with his own money,' and he goes on to ask: 'Why should the Jewish communities in America pay for his ticket across the Atlantic? It is not the Jewish purpose. The National purpose must have a priority.'

In the late 1970s tens of thousands of Soviet Jews, whose Communist education had allowed them not even an introduction to the concept of free choice, found themselves in Vienna confronted with a luxury they had not hitherto known. This, their first choice, was also the crucial decision of their lives. Many refuseniks who wanted to go to Israel spoke to me with understanding of this 'drop-out' phenomenon. A few, however, were bitter that most of those who chose to go from Vienna to the United States had never participated in the struggle for the right to emigrate. The battle had been fought on their behalf by those who were still not allowed to leave: a battle intended for Israel.

So the debate continues. The Jewish national purpose, one refusenik declares, is to go to Israel. The Jews *are* a nation. By going to Israel they are fulfilling their national goals. Soviet Jews, in applying for visas, are seeking only the repatriation which every nation grants to the nationals of other countries. But once America is the goal, he argues, the national purpose dissolves.

We leave the snow-filled night and return to the warmth of the small apartment. The blackboard on the sitting room wall is ready for the next Hebrew lesson. On the stove, pancakes have been prepared, and with them an invitingly sweet strawberry jam. The samovar is filled. The debate goes on.

The national movement of Jews to their land: this is the centre of refusenik thought and aspirations. How to maintain it? How to strengthen it? 'Those who studied the most Hebrew, the most Jewish history, the most Bible, it is they who fought to go to Israel – not to go to Brooklyn.' 'Let those who want to go to Brooklyn start their own fight.' 'They should not use Israel in this way.'

The debaters, despite the intensity of their own national aspirations, are realists. 'We accept that the majority of those who get visas for Israel will not stay on in Israel, even with direct flights. We want to change the balance, that is all.' 'We have had evidence that *one* conversation in a positive way changed a person's mind – even before he reached Israel. After all, these people haven't had a chance to know anything about Israel –

not even the simple things.'

The speakers are young men and women who have never had the opportunity, or the right, to read what they please, to listen to radio broadcasts without jamming, to study foreign newspapers, to correspond openly about the complexities and opportunities of life in Israel, or elsewhere. Their debates have all taken place in the half-light of partial knowledge and incomplete information. But, as Jews, they have absorbed the concept of a Jewish identity.

For the 10,000 and more refuseniks, and for tens of thousands of other Soviet Jews who have not yet taken the step into 'refusal', the concept of repatriation, reunification with their people, gives them the strength to live through an otherwise purposeless, and harassed, daily life. As one refusenik remarks to me, of the prospect of going to Israel: 'It filled the empty spaces for me.'

The Soviet authorities do their utmost to counter the emotional attraction of a distant land which no Soviet Jew has seen. One weapon has been put into their hands by the Jews themselves. It is part of the very openness of Israeli life: the moan. Graphic, sustained and, in Israel itself, a normal feature even of a contented existence, criticism abounds, of every aspect of life and society. As one refusenik puts it to me: 'Those from Israel complain,' 'those' being the long and vivid letters from former Soviet Jews, letters filled with the inevitable complaints of a newcomer, and even a not-so-newcomer, in a country where everyone considers himself an expert, even a potential Prime Minister.

These letters of complaint are vexatious in several different ways. While reflecting the natural tendency of any critic to exaggerate his tale, they make no reference to the many things which the writer in fact finds pleasant, or even admirable. They also serve as a dampening agent upon their recipients who, still in the Soviet Union, are unused to such outspokenness. Most serious of all, these letters give the Soviet authorities superb propaganda material, which they do not hesitate to use, to prove that life in Israel is nasty, vicious and cruel.

'Those from Israel complain,' my refusenik friend repeats. 'But those from the United States don't complain, because they are ashamed. There, everybody *must* succeed. If they don't succeed, it's their own fault.' As for those Soviet Jews who go to Israel, many, almost as soon as they arrive, '. . . start to forget everything they had here. Even in Vienna they phone and say things they would never have dreamed of saying on the telephone. They forget even how dangerous it used to be to talk openly on the telephone.'

The refusenik leaders understand this phenomenon all too well. Without having seen Vienna, Tel Aviv or New York, they recognize the temptations and distortions each of these cities and cultures can implant. They can be bitter too about 'the lack of responsibility', the 'lack of balance', of the Soviet Jew who, freed from the formidable restraints of Soviet society, succumbs to the luxury of western criticism and denunciation. But, strange as it may seem, bitterness is not a predominant characteristic of the refuseniks. If it were, they would long ago have succumbed to despair. Instead, a maturity of judgement leads to an understanding even of these letters of complaint. 'We see from these letters', I was told, 'that it *is* my homeland; like to our mother, one tells all one's troubles.'

'We just want to buy a ticket . . . .'

Here in the Soviet Union, among Soviet Jews, when a particularly sensitive issue has to be discussed, or a name mentioned, or a telephone number transferred, no word is spoken. 'We live under great stress,' comments one of those, a leader, who lives under daily pressure. 'The walls have ears – and the ceilings too.' Instead of speaking about sensitive matters, a few refuseniks prefer to produce a child's writing slate, a 'magic screen' on which to write, show to a guest, and then rub out. On one occasion I was present at a conversation which took place on a blackboard. The entire conversation was carried on in chalk. The 'chip, chip, chip' of the chalk on the board was as expressive as any movement of the lips.

Openly or secretly, the message is the same. Again and again I was asked to transmit it. 'We are not, and do not intend to become, critics or opponents of the Soviet Government. We are not dissidents. We are not agents of any foreign power. We are Soviet citizens, loyal to the State, fulfilling all our obligations as citizens, and seeking to fulfil our aspirations within the framework of Soviet law.'

The debate comes to an end. The participants set off to their homes. But saying farewell is painful. I, who can fly to Israel tomorrow, shake hands with the men and women who have been refused that right for many years. The Soviet system is so strong, yet it does not feel strong enough to let them go.

As the tea cups are put away, and the samovar emptied, my host of the evening remarks, with a rare passion: 'We don't want their power. We don't want their wealth. We just want to buy a ticket to go to our country.'

7

Repatriation

———◇———

A quiet street in a Moscow suburb. The way to Yuly
Kosharovsky's apartment on Gerasima Kurina Street
leads past a railway embankment. Night has just fallen,
and through the darkness can be heard the sound of a
train, coming from the direction of the city. In a moment
it is chuntering past, the lights in its windows like warm
fires, teasing the cold night. Then it is gone, the clatter of
its wheels receding into silence.

The train is the 17.58 night express from Moscow to
Berlin. On certain nights, through-carriages continue
westwards to Paris, to Brussels and to Ostend. At
Ostend there is a connecting cross-Channel boat to
Britain. Every night of the year, the express passes this
spot, and every night, if he chances by at this hour, Yuly
Kosharovsky can look up at its lights, and just make out,
on its side, the destination board of cities he can never
visit.

Never? He first asked for an exit visa on 10 March
1971, at the age of twenty-nine. The savage verdicts of
the Leningrad trials had not deterred him, any more
than they had deterred thousands of other young Jews,
from putting in their applications. Kosharovsky was

refused a visa.

But he did not give up, his second application being submitted on 12 May 1973. He was then told that, if unsuccessful, the re-application procedure must be repeated every six months. Each application requires new documents, new proof that the applicant has been 'invited' to Israel, new evidence that he has no relatives in the Soviet Union who do not wish him to leave.

Kosharovsky's first refusal was on the grounds of 'secrecy'. Until his application, he had been a radio electronics engineer. In 1974, after his second application, he was told that the 'secrecy' restrictions had been removed. His second refusal had been as a 'punishment' for being an 'activist'. Two subsequent applications were rejected, the reasons being given as 'State secrets' and 'secrecy', although he had been unable to continue work in his profession since his first application, and had done no 'secret' work in electronics since 1968.

Since first applying for a visa, Kosharovsky has been denied the right to practise his profession, and has had to work instead in various menial jobs, first of all as a nightwatchman in a cinema. In the summer of 1975 he started a seminar for unemployed engineers. Warned to stop this seminar, he refused. Sentenced on two separate occasions to fifteen days in prison, for 'hooliganism' and 'disturbing public order', his telephone was disconnected. His wife Inna, a mathematics student from Moscow State University, has never been allowed to practise in her field.

Shortly after the Soviet ratification of the Helsinki Agreement on 18 September 1975, Kosharovsky was among a group of some sixty refuseniks who went to the Central Committee building in Moscow, convinced that the Agreement ought to be implemented in favour of their applications to leave. To the amazement of the refuseniks present, six of the group were invited to discuss the matter with the Chief of the Administrative Department of the Central Committee, Comrade Albert Ivanov, and the Chairman of the Visa Department, Colonel Obidin.

Kosharovsky was one of the six Jews chosen to represent their fellow refuseniks. The other five were Mark Azbel, Vitali Rubin, Victor Brailovsky, Alexander Lerner and Vladimir Slepak. They presented their grievances, which the officials rejected. Obidin went so far as to tell the group that the provisions of the Helsinki Agreement relating to the reunification of families actually *narrowed* their chances of emigration, rather than broadening them. 'Family', Obidin insisted, comprised no one but next of kin.

In the next eight years, of the six refuseniks in the delegation, only Azbel and Rubin were to receive visas. Brailovsky and Slepak were to face the full rigours of the criminal code.

Kosharovsky continued to seek the right to emigrate for all fellow Jews, and was brought together in friendship with several other activists, among them Vladimir Slepak and Yosif Begun. Together, these friends worked to encourage others, and to challenge the growing number of refusals. The bonds of friendship grew, giving strength as well as comradeship.

On 10 March 1978, the seventh anniversary of his first application, Kosharovsky wrote direct to the Secretary General of the Communist Party, Leonid Brezhnev. In his letter he pointed out how unfairly the 'secrecy' reason had been used against him. Having graduated

Repatriation

from the Ural Polytechnical Institute in 1965, he explained, he had been sent to the Automatics Research Institute in Sverdlovsk. The work had been given 'second grade security clearance'. This meant that he had 'no right to contact foreigners or to go overseas' until three years after the security clearance had expired.

In 1968, Kosharovsky told Brezhnev, 'I resigned from the Institute.' In the following ten years he had no contact with any secret work. 'Thus, at the moment, the term of my "quarantine" is three and a half times longer than the one specified in the regulations.'

Kosharovsky went on to point out to Brezhnev that, prior to his first application for a visa, he had visited his former superior at the Automatics Research Institute, A. Filkin, who told him 'that, in fact, the "secrecy" had expired even earlier', because of the 'quick obsoleteness' of the work which he had been doing when he left the Institute.

Kosharovsky then set out for Brezhnev the international documents on which he based his application: the statement in the Universal Declaration of Human Rights that 'Everyone has the right to leave any country, including his own', and the Final Act of the Helsinki Conference on Security and Co-operation in Europe, upholding that right, as signed in Helsinki on 1 August 1975, ratified by the Presidium of the Supreme Soviet in Moscow on 18 September 1975, and coming into effect on 23 March 1976.

'In view of the above', Kosharovsky added, 'I consider the seven-year-long refusal to grant me and my family the exit visa to be an act of tyranny.' He also considered, he said, 'the conditions in which my family had been made to live' was likewise 'an act of tyranny'.

The Jews of Hope

In 1971, he pointed out, a book published in 1925 by the Soviet writer Maxim Gorky, *Against the Anti-Semites*, had been confiscated from him, and never returned. During President Nixon's first visit to Moscow in 1975 he had been imprisoned for fifteen days in Volokolamsk prison, 'where I was subjected to cruel and humiliating treatment – they twisted my arms, placed me in a "box", threatened me with physical reprisal'. During the Moscow Symposium on Jewish Culture in December 1976 he had been placed under house-arrest 'while I was sick, and was deprived of the possibility to receive medical care'.

Kosharovsky also pointed out to Brezhnev that in the Soviet television film *Traders of Souls*, shown in Moscow and elsewhere on 22 January 1977, 'I was groundlessly accused of conspiratorial activities and connection with international imperialism'. In accordance with Article 7 of the Civil Code of the Russian Soviet Republic, he had applied to the People's Court for permission to bring a legal case against the television company, to protect his 'honour and dignity'. His application had been rejected, but without any reason. Such a rejection, Kosharovsky noted, was a 'violation of Article 129 of the Civil Procedure Code'.

Kosharovsky's appeal to Brezhnev was in vain. Not only was he still refused an exit visa, but his Hebrew teaching was not recognized as legitimate work. In order to have it 'legitimized', he applied for permission to pay income tax on his earnings from teaching. This application was refused, and he was told that unless he obtained 'proper' employment, he would be charged with 'parasitism', a criminal offence.

In March 1980 Kosharovsky obtained work as a

janitor in a kindergarten. His earnings were then 70 roubles a month. In the evenings, and on Sundays, he continued to give private Hebrew lessons.

In June 1980, Kosharovsky's continued application for an exit visa seemed, momentarily, to take a positive turn. For in that month, his wife Inna, summoned to the Visa Office, was told that her husband's secrecy classification had been cancelled. But bad news followed immediately. There was still no point in his applying again, said the official. There was now a new reason for his refusal: he has no close relatives in Israel. At the age of forty, Kosharovsky was suddenly confronted with a new excuse, and a blank wall.

The question of kinship in Israel raises a central issue of Jewish emigration. Two separate justifications for emigration give Soviet Jews the legal right to leave. Both are embodied in the Helsinki Agreement to which Kosharovsky had referred in his letter to Brezhnev, and which specifically endorsed the post-war Universal Declaration of Human Rights. According to this Declaration: 'Everyone has the right to leave any country, including his own, and to return to his country.' An additional article of the Helsinki Agreement states: 'Everyone shall be free to leave any country including his own.'

The 'right to leave', and the right to be 'free to leave': both these pledges were endorsed by the Soviet Union. Neither depends in any way upon a close degree of kinship, or upon relatives living abroad. Both pledges are unqualified expressions of what the Helsinki Agreement calls 'fundamental freedoms'.

Tragically for Soviet Jews, even those families who do have a part of their family in Israel are often denied permission to leave. Yet even here, the Helsinki Agreement pledged the participating States to deal 'in a humanitarian spirit with the applications of persons who wish to be reunited with members of their families'.

Hundreds of divided families are still denied the right to be together, while those who have no close family link are told that the lack of such a link constitutes a veto on emigration. Actually, by the Helsinki Agreement, the mere desire to leave is sufficient reason to be allowed to leave. 'Everyone has the right to leave any country including his own.' These words are engraved on the hearts of those ten thousand Jews whose application to leave has been rejected, and the many thousands more who would certainly apply to go if this right were to be upheld.

There is another bitter twist in the refusenik situation. The Universal Declaration of Human Rights stipulates the right of the individual 'to leave any country, including his own *and to return to his country*'. The words in italics hold a particular irony for the refuseniks. As they see it, they are seeking not only to leave their 'own' country, the Soviet Union, but 'to return' to their country, Israel. As Jews, identified in their Soviet documents as Jewish by 'nationality', they regard Israel as their true national centre and national home. They therefore feel a double legality in their request to leave the Soviet Union: the right to leave, and the right to return. They wish to leave the one, and to return to the other.

For Yuly Kosharovsky, and for many like him who have been told that they do not have close enough kin in Israel, the terms of the 1948 Universal Declaration of Human Rights, and of the 1975 Helsinki Agreement, are of overriding legal importance. Nor do they stand alone.

The right to emigrate has been enshrined in so many international instruments, and has been given such widespread and frequent expression, that it may properly be considered a part of customary international law. This right is first asserted in Article 13(2) of the 1948 Universal Declaration of Human Rights, which states: 'Everyone has the right to leave any country, including his own, and to return to his country.' This same right finds expression in Article 2 of the 1963 Protocol No. 4 to the European Convention for the Protection of Human Rights and Fundamental Freedoms; in Article 5(d) of the 1965 International Convention on the Elimination of all Forms of Racial Discrimination; in Article 12(2) of the 1966 International Covenant on Civil and Political Rights, which stipulates: 'Everyone shall be free to leave any country, including his own'; in Article 22 of the 1969 American Convention on Human Rights; and in the 1975 Final Act of the Helsinki Conference on Security and Co-operation in Europe.

Because the right to emigrate freely has become a part of customary international law, the Soviet Union, as a member of the international community, would be obliged to respect this right even if it were not a party to a single international treaty dealing with the subject. The Soviet Union has expressly endorsed the right to free emigration, however, through its adherence to international treaties on the subject; it has even gone beyond this, incorporating the right to emigrate in its own domestic law.

Kosharovsky has applied to go to Israel, and his application has been refused. His demand is: repatriation, the return of a people to its land, the return of the Jew to Israel. Denied this right, he continued to teach Hebrew, the language of the Jewish people and the Jewish State. 'It is not simply the language itself,' he wrote. 'It is the essence of my life, ever since my professional life was disrupted.' The lessons themselves, he adds, 'are within the law. In fact, I have in the past invited them to come and listen to us, if they suspect anything. I went even further. I invited them to give us a room in their Club and appoint overseers. We've been *forced* to teach in private homes.' Kosharovsky adds: 'You're allowed to study Chinese or English, even though relations with China and America are not too warm. Why can't we study Hebrew? It's open discrimination.'

On 15 July 1980 Kosharovsky was 'invited' to a Moscow police station, where three KGB men spoke to him for four hours. Their tone was 'polite'. But their message was ominous. First they showed him a large cardboard box filled with letters, and told him that all these letters had been signed by him, and that they could arrest him straight away, using the letters as the basis for criminal charges. Then they read aloud a few extracts from the letters, arguing – falsely – that they represented an attempt by Kosharovsky to organize in the West an economic and political boycott against the Soviet Union.

The three KGB men then played Kosharovsky a tape-recording, stating that it was an interview which he had given to a western tourist. It was impossible either to recognize who was speaking in the recording, or what was being said. Nevertheless, the KGB men insisted that it was indeed Kosharovsky and a foreign visitor, and that the interview contained anti-Soviet propaganda.

It would be easy enough, the KGB men declared, to 'create' evidence against him, if they wished. To avoid such a fate, he should stop teaching Hebrew.

'Does your approach reflect the official point of view?' Kosharovsky asked his three interrogators.

'You have two months at your disposal,' they answered. 'Once the two months have passed, we will start taking measures.'

Exactly two months later, on 15 September 1980, while Kosharovsky was on holiday in the Crimea, 'an incident took place', as he later complained to the KGB, 'which left no doubts in my mind about the sources of it'. Getting up at 7.30 in the morning to do his morning jogging, 'I noticed nearby a man walking about somewhat unsteadily and carrying a bottle of wine wrapped in a newspaper. My friends saw this man a long time before I came out. He waited patiently while I limbered up and when I started running he moved towards me, deliberately walking unsteadily. Despite the fact that I ran at a distance of about one and a half metres away from him, he managed to swing in such a way that he touched me and then immediately dropped the bottle. After that his behaviour became very noisy and aggressive. A couple of minutes later, two healthy-looking fellows who were standing not far away and who introduced themselves as *druzhinniki* (members of the People's Guard) came up to us. They quickly "pacified" the noisy stranger but, nevertheless, took us both to the police station and stated that there had been a quarrel.'

Kosharovsky and his assailant were then driven to another town, some miles away. There, he and the 'noisy stranger' were sentenced to thirteen days in prison.

Kosharovsky was imprisoned. The stranger managed somehow to 'disappear' even before the verdict was read, and did not serve his sentence.

Kosharovsky returned to Moscow, and to his Hebrew lessons. Then, on 12 December 1980, while he was on his way to a pupil, he was stopped in the street by the KGB, taken to the police station, and warned that if he continued to give Hebrew lessons he would be 'the next after Brailovsky': a reference to the arrest a month earlier of another leading refusenik, Victor Brailovsky. The warnings continued for three hours, until the period of the lessons had passed. Meanwhile, several of Kosharovsky's pupils were warned that they were 'in danger of being corrupted' by their teacher.

Three times more, Kosharovsky was arrested on his way to give Hebrew lessons. On 25 February 1981 a KGB man told him that if he continued to try to go to his lessons, 'we will break your hands and feet'. He would not, he was told, get to his lessons 'even through the drainpipe'. In vain, he appealed to the Moscow Procurator's Office: 'Protect me.'

Kosharovsky continued to teach Hebrew, and his pupils to progress under his expert guidance. Then, on 4 March 1981, he was called yet again to the KGB. Unless he stopped his 'activities', he was told, he would be beaten up by 'street hooligans', and sent to prison. Two days later he received a telephone call from the KGB. 'We have finished off the "dissidents",' he was told. 'There are no more religious "activists" threatening the regime. Who remain? You Jews. And among the Jews are their cultural bodies. We know that there are no actual establishments. But there are individuals who study, who teach. We'll do away with all that.'

Repatriation

It had become physically impossible for Kosharovsky to continue his Hebrew lessons. Now it was the turn of his pupils, who were themselves giving lessons to others, to be threatened.

In 1983 Kosharovsky was working as a repairman, fixing television sets. His daily life continued without a visa, and without being able to teach Hebrew. His home remained a place of hope, and a place of joy. His first son, Eliezer, known as 'Eli', had been born on 10 September 1978, his second son, Matityahu, known as 'Mati', on 22 June 1981.

On 15 October 1981, three months after Mati's birth, the KGB conducted a twelve-hour search of Kosharovsky's apartment, taking away his radio, his tape-recorder, batteries, plugs, a camera, a photographic enlarger and some English novels.

Under Soviet law, each Article of which the refuseniks know so well, the only material that can be confiscated is that which is to be used as evidence in a trial. But there was no trial; nor was the material returned. Three days after the raid, Kosharovsky wrote a letter of protest to the then Chairman of the KGB, Yury Andropov, giving details of the threats that had been made by the KGB in Moscow, and during his holiday in the Crimea. 'I therefore ask you most urgently', he wrote, 'to look into this matter and to punish those responsible.' Kosharovsky received no reply.

Each Friday night Inna Kosharovsky lights the Sabbath candles. How well I recall the scene on one such occasion: the small kitchen filled with laughter. Mikhail, her eldest son by a previous marriage, sits with his girl friend. Mati, the youngest boy, plays on a swing hung up in a doorway, while his brother Eli seeks to catch his

103

father's attention by showing off his latest toy, a wooden woodpecker. These family scenes, caught by the cameras of two visitors – myself and my friend Jonathan Wootliff – were among several hundred photographs of refuseniks and their families which the Soviet authorities insisted upon developing themselves, and then confiscated before forwarding the regular tourist 'snaps'. For reasons known only to the Soviet State, Mati and Eli are not to be seen abroad.

Like so many refuseniks, the Kosharovskys hope that their knowledge of the Hebrew language will serve them well once they are citizens in Israel. But even the right to learn Hebrew is constantly under pressure. Other Soviet citizens may learn whatever language they choose. Soviet language academies are famous for their high standards, whether of English or Hindi. In the few Institutes where Hebrew is taught in the Soviet Union, it is limited to a few Christian priests and 'special' students, almost none of them Jews but in many cases KGB agents training to be Jewish 'experts'. There are no official Hebrew schools, no Hebrew newspapers, no Hebrew publishing houses. Nor are any Hebrew records made in the Soviet Union.

In trying to teach Hebrew, Soviet Jews seek no special privilege. 'We want cultural equality with the rest of the people who inhabit this country,' Kosharovsky explains, 'no more, no less: the right to study our traditions, our religion, our language. Every other "nationality" in the Soviet Union has such a right.' This is so. Armenians are taught Armenian, Ukrainians study Ukrainian, Latvians speak Latvian. The Jews are the only officially designated nationality denied this right.

In one of the searches of Kosharovsky's apartment,

the right to study Hebrew was clearly challenged when his Hebrew-language books were taken away: 'not my Japanese books and not my Arabic books: no other languages but Hebrew. It was a clear denial of that right.' The searchers also took two seventeenth-century Bibles, and a copy of Lenin's article on the National Question. 'I asked for it back. Nothing was returned.'

Each Hebrew teacher has different pressures and harassments to recount. After one of his classes, Kosharovsky's neighbours protested to the Militia. 'See what a Zionist centre you have here,' they complained. Speaking 'foreign languages' in the lift or stairwell is another frequent complaint made by 'concerned citizens'.

The teachers are not so easily bullied, arguing that they have their rights under Soviet law, even when they receive Hebrew-language text books from abroad. As Kosharovsky explained, 'a free exchange of cultural ideas, the receiving of language books, not ideological ones, is completely within the framework of Soviet law, and within the practice of the Soviet authorities towards other nations'.

Why should the sending in of Hebrew grammars and dictionaries be seen as such a threat to the Soviet authorities? The writer Y. L. Peretz once explained that the Hebrew language was 'the cement which binds together our scattered units'.

When Peretz wrote these words he was a subject of the Tsar. Since then, the Hebrew language has gained a further appeal for the scattered Jews, as the daily language of the Jewish State. 'Hebrew', Peretz wrote, 'is the tongue of our religion and nationality.' Soviet Jews are inscribed as a 'nationality' in their internal passport.

The Jews of Hope

They ask only to be treated as one, even in the matter of learning languages. Yet when the officials threaten those who teach Hebrew, 'the charge', as Kosharovsky points out, 'is always anti-Soviet activity. But how', he goes on to ask, 'can a Hebrew-English dictionary contain anti-Soviet activity?' The authorities have an answer even to that question. As Kosharovsky was told after the Hebrew-English dictionaries and the Hebrew grammars had been seized: 'This is Zionist propaganda.'

———◇———

The life of a refusenik, Kosharovsky comments, 'is like waiting in a railway station. You expect the train at any moment. You don't pay attention to the future. You expect your train any time.' More than a decade has passed for Kosharovsky on that station platform. But his train is still nowhere in sight.

The discussion turns to the question of Jews who have been refused their visas again and again, some for more than ten years. Ought there not to be some agreed time limit to how long a person can be refused a visa? Kosharovsky is now in his twelfth year of 'refusal'. Might there not be some agreed, tacit maximum number of years, whereby he and those like him would already have been allowed to leave long ago?

The discussion of such questions is a daily feature of refusenik life. The answers are less forthcoming: indeed, it seems impossible to obtain any answers at all. At the age of forty-one, Kosharovsky has now been denied for more than a decade the chance of contributing his professional skills to Soviet society. Can he not be allowed to make his contribution, albeit belatedly, to modern Israel? He is a man of humane and liberal instincts, who has much to give any society that values his qualities, and recognizes his courage. Now he tries to work out some ground rules, whereby emigration could begin again, and on a more regular, open basis.

Four developments seem to Kosharovsky to be worth urging: first, a limit to the time taken by the process of application. At present it can take up to two years merely to process an application. But once an application is accepted, people have to pay all their debts, sell most of their belongings, prepare the myriad details of emigration. A long drawn out process of application causes havoc to this process. Yet according to Soviet law, an answer ought to be given within one month. 'What is now needed', Kosharovsky suggests, 'is a decision of the Supreme Soviet to limit acceptance of any application to one month.'

A second barrier to emigration is the Soviet insistence upon a written invitation from Israel. But, Kosharovsky asks, as the Israel Government's own Law of Return does not require an invitation, why should the Soviets require one? If they were to allow direct flights from Moscow to Tel Aviv, perhaps through some Communist capital such as Bucharest, which already has flights to Israel, the authorities would know that all visa-holders were on their way to Israel. They would need no formal invitation to prove it.

A third point which troubles all refuseniks is that with each new application, a Soviet Jew must also submit a written document from his or her closest relatives in the Soviet Union, stating that they have no objection to the exit visa.

Having to write such a document even once can be risky for a relative, a father or a brother. Having to sign this document for each re-application can be an increasing risk. In addition, as Kosharovsky points out, the relative may not be on particularly close terms, may live thousands of miles away within the Soviet Union, and may be unwilling to take the risk once, let alone once every six months. This little-known relative might even sympathize with the official Soviet view. So the need for these constantly renewed documents after the first refusal can be a strong hindrance, even a decisive barrier, to future applications.

A fourth hindrance which Kosharovsky feels should be the subject of some formal agreement is the cost of emigration. High taxes are charged for the right to leave, and for the obligatory renunciation of citizenship, making the cost to a husband and wife with two children, including travel tickets, at least 3,000 roubles. But few refuseniks earn more than 150 roubles a month. And there are other charges to be considered; to take his books overseas an emigrant must pay a tax equivalent to the original cost of each book: that is to say, he must pay for his books over again.

Kosharovsky's own large array of books has been diminished by raids; even so, he would find it difficult financially to take out those that remain.

Above all, in the view of many refuseniks, the emphasis must be taken away from the issue of divided families, of whom there are relatively few, to that of repatriation. 'If you don't have close relatives in Israel,' says Kosharovsky, 'you still want to be part of that nation.'

More than any other single event since the foundation of the State of Israel in 1948, it was the Six-Day War of 1967, when Israel defeated three armies, Egyptian,

Syrian and Jordanian, that created a new spirit of national identification among Soviet Jews. Most Soviet Jews had previously felt no identification at all with the Jewish State. As Kosharovsky explains: 'During the Six-Day War the Soviet newspapers said Israel was being crushed. That thousands of Israelis were dead. That Israel was being swept away in an Arab sea. I made a big antenna in my house to try to get information. I couldn't. I felt a blow. I wanted to die with my people.' But then the official news changed. Israel had won, but only as the aggressor, using overwhelming force against a defenceless foe. 'It was a clear lie against my people.'

Hundreds of thousands of Soviet Jews were electrified by Israel's victory in the 1967 war. But it was the shrill Soviet propaganda about Israel's imminent and total defeat that ignited the fuse of national identity. Some recall that this propaganda was so gloating in tone as to heighten to its limit the sense of affinity with the apparently doomed State. From that moment, many Soviet Jews regarded Israel as their nation, and emigration to Israel as their national purpose.

8

Anti-Semitism

———◇———

The majority of the refuseniks whom I met had a sense of humour which their six-, ten- or even twelve-year struggle for a visa had done nothing to dim. Pinned to the bookcases of several of those whom I visited was a neatly written copy of an official Soviet decree dated 27 June 1918. This decree, published in the Communist Party newspaper *Izvestia*, was a denunciation of anti-Semitism. Its tough final paragraph was drafted by Lenin himself, and reads: 'The Council of People's Commissars instructs all Soviet deputies to take uncompromising measures to tear the anti-Semitic movement out by the roots. Pogromists and pogrom-agitators are to be placed outside the law.'

All Soviet Jews, whether or not they aspire to leave, would like to feel that anti-Semitism is a thing of the past, a memory of bygone Tsarist years, a curiosity of long-gone decades. Yet, even during my own short visit to the Soviet Union, there were many indications, almost daily indications, that traditional anti-Jewish attitudes are not dead; that they are being deliberately stirred up in order to create a gulf between those Soviet Jews who wish to emigrate, and the rest of Soviet society.

Anti-Semitism

On 28 February 1983, two days before my own journey to the Soviet Union, the Ukrainian newspaper *Molodezh Ukrainy* published an article which made a strong attack on Jews wishing to leave the Soviet Union. The article was based upon the alleged complaints of Soviet Jews who had reached Israel and become rapidly disillusioned. Jews who went to Israel went to 'an alien world', the article declared. They lost 'that which is most dear – their Homeland'. Those Jews who reached Israel found that the 'cheerful cock-and-bull stories' about wealth and the easy life were 'quickly smashed on the rock of cruel reality'. But this was the 'natural retribution for carelessness and for treason'.

The right of the individual to leave any country for any other country had become 'treason': a particularly harsh accusation for Soviet readers, in whom loyalty to their State is constantly instilled as the highest virtue.

Not only the behaviour of individual Jews in the 1980s, but their behaviour a century earlier, is questioned in current Soviet publications. My arrival in the Soviet Union also coincided with an article in the popular Leningrad history magazine *Neva* which made the astonishing claim that stories of the persecution of the Jews under the Tsars were nothing but 'Zionist propaganda'. According to the article, the much-publicized pogroms of the Tsarist era arose, not from any irrational Jew hatred, but because the Jews themselves had provoked local and peasant anger by their economic dominance. No mention was made of the fact that much of Jewish life in the Pale of Settlement was marked by extreme poverty.

This particular article went on to assert that in Russia 'it was always good for Jews'. To say otherwise, the

111

article reiterated, 'is a Zionist lie'.

Such assertions are officially inspired. Statements which appear in the Soviet press do not indicate the personal opinion of the writer, but are a direct reflection of the official view, intended to be taken seriously. Their tone is meant to be reflected in the subsequent attitude of their readers, and such articles are frequently reprinted in various forms in different types of newspapers: in mass circulation weeklies, in Army and Air Force papers, in provincial papers and in youth magazines.

Twenty years ago, and throughout the earlier post-revolutionary decades, it was the emphatic assertion of Soviet historians that life in pre-revolutionary Russia was a prison. Now, Soviet citizens are told, it was not so bad for the Jews. Somehow, inexplicably, the 'Zionists' and the pre-revolutionary Jewish Social Democratic Party were, it appears, exempt from the 'evils' of Tsardom, against which Lenin struggled. It is not mentioned, nor explained, that Jews were in the forefront of the revolutionary as well as the Zionist movement, a most inconvenient fact if Jews were not 'in fact' the victims of Tsarist oppression.

Inevitably, Jews in the Soviet Union today are sensitive to such distortion, and to the efforts made in the press, in books and elsewhere to portray them as alien from the true pattern of Soviet historic experience, life and aspirations. The method used is both a denial of Jewish historic suffering, and a linking of Jewish national aspirations with an alleged sinister Zionist conspiracy to undermine the Soviet Union. 'Zionism' – which for Soviet Jews means only the wish to be a part of the Jewish national home – is portrayed as a sinister force, whose tentacles have spread out from the Middle

112

East to the very heart of mother Russia: a source not only of corruption, but of treason.

Each week, and at times almost daily, press articles, television programmes and wall posters portray Israel as a brutal, even a neo-Nazi State. It is a deliberate attempt, one refusenik commented, 'to try to create a revulsion in Jewish minds, a revulsion against going to Israel'.

This Nazi-Israel link had been made explicit three weeks before my visit, on 11 February 1983, in the Kiev newspaper *Robochaya Gazeta*. In an article entitled 'Zionism, Illusion and reality', with the subtitle 'Following Goebbels' Recipes', the writer A. Svidnitsky stated, in explanation of what he called Israel's 'pre-planned genocide' in the Lebanon, that 'several dozen former SS officers, pupils of the Hitler Youth, taught in Israeli para-military schools and prepared specialists in conducting punitive expeditions'.

Svidnitsky's article continued: 'The Zionist six-pointed Star of David has replaced the spider-like swastika. Zionism is the new Fascism, which encompasses the Near East with barbed-wire and dreams about new conquests of territory. But the judgement of the nations will come for hangmen guilty of genocide . . . .'

Like all newspaper accusations, this one was not only read by those citizens who bought the newspaper, but by a far larger number who read it on the many street display boards, on which newspapers are pinned up for all to see, and to study.

For the 10,000 Soviet Jews who have been refused permission to go to Israel, this direct and public linking of Zionism with Nazism is not only deeply offensive, but is a grave personal threat. For, by such assertions, those

Jews who wish to go to Israel are equated with the most hated historic enemy of the Russian people.

Even the wartime suffering of the Jews is used to strengthen this equation. While the Nazis were burning 'thousands of Jews' in the 'furnaces of the concentration camps', Svidnitsky informed his readers, 'Zionist agents also more than once concluded deals with the Hitlerites regarding the removal of people needed by them from Germany and Austria'. The reason for these alleged 'deals' was that 'the Zionists needed youths drilled in the Nazi manner, prepared to fight without hesitation for the class interests of the Jewish rich'.

For a Soviet Jew who seeks to go to Israel, these allegations are frightening and ominous. How well I remember sitting with two refuseniks one morning when the telephone rang, and a fellow refusenik asked: 'Have you read the article in yesterday's Moscow evening newspaper?' No, neither of them had done so. The friend quickly gave them the gist of it, and they blenched. By late that afternoon I had a copy of it in my hand.

Like so many such articles, it was crude and vicious in its language, making no attempt at subtlety. Ostensibly a book review, it left Muscovites in no doubt as to who their enemies were: first, so-called tourists who had in fact been sent to the Soviet Union by 'foreign Intelligence'. Behind these 'tourists' was, first and foremost, the Central Intelligence Agency in Washington, 'misusing' the Helsinki Agreement by infiltrating these 'tourists' in order 'to recruit agents among renegades and corrupt individuals who are outcasts from Soviet society – who have not found a place in our Soviet family . . .'.

Examples of these outcasts were then given: two of

them were refuseniks, Anatoly Shcharansky – serving thirteen years 'deprivation of liberty' – and his friend Vladimir Slepak, recently released after five years in exile. According to the article, Slepak, although now at liberty, was a 'Zionist agent' working on behalf of the Israeli secret service, 'spreading slanderous anti-Soviet rumours among Soviet citizens of Jewish nationality in the Soviet Union', and 'organizing false invitations' to Israel.

Among the so-called 'traitors' listed in the article were several non-Jewish dissidents as well as Jewish refuseniks: all were said to be people who had 'betrayed their motherland'. During the war, the article stated, the collaborators who worked with Hitler were the enemies of the Soviet Union. Shcharansky, the article added, was 'of course' of a younger generation. But 'some years later' he too had betrayed 'the Soviet motherland'.

According to this article, the only difference between Shcharansky and the traitors of the Nazi era was that those who collaborated with the Nazis betrayed their motherland 'for the marks of Hitler's Reich', while today Shcharansky and others 'betray for United States dollars'. Then, the traitors worked for the Gestapo. Now they work for the Central Intelligence Agency.

Naturally, the article made no reference to the fact that, on 13 June 1977, more than a year before Shcharansky's trial, President Carter had publicly repudiated the fact that Shcharansky had worked as an agent for the United States Government, nor to the letter of the eighteen refuseniks from Minsk, among them Lev Ovsishcher and Gennady Feldman, who had written to Leonid Brezhnev that Shcharansky was only being brought to trial 'because he insisted on his unquestionable right to emigrate to Israel and because he helped others to obtain their rights'.

According to the allegations in the article, the 'betrayal' by Shcharansky and Slepak of their motherland could not be considered 'less villainous' than treachery by Soviet citizens during the war. 'That is the reason', the article ended, 'why the Soviet people completely approve the punishment that was given to these traitors.'

How do such allegations affect the average Soviet citizen, with his many other problems nearer home? One refusenik told me: 'In Moscow I cannot see any special growth of anti-Semitism in the street as a result of such articles. But in the Ukraine it is much worse. In the shops there, during my last visit, people were saying: "In the last war, from 1941 to 1945, Jews were just sitting quietly in Tashkent, more than a thousand miles away from the front line. They were cowards. But now that it is possible for Jews to kill women and children they are taking the opportunity to do so." I heard this myself in Kharkov . . . .'

This particular refusenik knew, as do almost all Soviet Jews, of the scale of Jewish participation in the war, and of the extent of Jewish suffering. In Kharkov itself, tens of thousands of Jews had been massacred. 'I don't know how bad a conscience people should have', comments one refusenik, 'after this tremendous tragedy. How dare they say such things about Tashkent, about cowardice.' And yet, she points out, these remarks are possible as a result of the Soviet educational system. 'They try to hide historical truth in the schools. They really are not taught anything about the holocaust.'

The deliberate linking of the Nazi era, Israel, and

Anti-Semitism

Soviet Jewry led some refuseniks I met to bitter reflections: 'How someone dares to compare Hitler and Israel, or the Nazis and us Zionists! These press articles are a very hard indicator that there is no hope and no future for the Jews *here*. But for western interest, western activity, maybe half of us would be hanged already.'

The Jews would also win through, however: 'It is always so during Jewish history. It is a pity only that for the Jews history is also not without victims. The cost is great from the Jewish side.'

However much Israel is denounced, the refuseniks do not waver in their support for its existence. Indeed, their own morale is strengthened by that existence. 'It was the creation of the State of Israel,' one refusenik told me in Moscow, 'which gave Russian Jews a focus against assimilation. Israel provided a feeling of identity, of common responsibility, of common goals.'

Week after week, however, Jewish national aspirations are portrayed in the Soviet press as evil and diseased. It was a popular writer, Lev Korneyev, who in a book review in *Komsomolskaya Pravda*, published while I was in Moscow on 1 March 1983, stated that the meaning of Zionism was 'to turn every Jew, no matter where he lives, into an agent of the Jewish oligarchy, into a traitor to the country where he was born'.

Korneyev's accusation, published in a newspaper read by hundreds of thousands of Young Communists and would-be Communists, turns the national aspirations even of teenage Soviet Jews into a crime against the Soviet Union.

Writings such as those of Korneyev find an echo in physical acts. At the beginning of April 1983 news circulated in refusenik circles in Moscow of the desecration of 200 Jewish graves in the cemetery of Chernovtsy, in the Ukraine. This was 'a bad omen', one refusenik explained, since 'nothing happens in the Ukraine without the permission of the Soviet authorities in the Kremlin'. Indeed, he added, anti-Semitic acts are often 'tested' in the Ukraine first. To those refuseniks who see the situation as 'very gloomy and dark', this graveyard desecration was a further 'ominous sign' of a revival of pressure and prejudice.

In June 1983 the misrepresentation of Jewish history and Zionism reached a climax with the publication of a new book by Lev Korneyev, *The Class Essence of Zionism*. Wherever Jews lived outside Israel, according to Korneyev, they represented a potentially subversive 'fifth column'. The establishment of a Jewish homeland in Israel gave rise to the 'dual loyalty' of Jews living outside Israel. This concept of 'dual loyalty' was widely exploited by the Israeli Government for spying purposes, and in the interests of American imperialism, world war and international terrorism.

Jewish monopolists and bankers seek today to dominate the world through political and economic subterfuge, Korneyev wrote, just as, in the 1930s Jewish bankers and industrialists 'conspired' to keep Hitler in power, with the aim of establishing a Jewish State in Palestine. In the nineteenth century Jews 'brought pogroms upon themselves' in order to stimulate emigration. In the 1930s Zionist leaders and Jewish bankers 'helped Hitler prepare for the seizure of power, even though they knew of Hitler's intention to exterminate the Jews'.

'It is known', Korneyev added, 'that the extermination of hundreds of thousands of Jews is one of the main arguments for Zionism, which the Zionists – supporters of the Nazis – cynically exploit for their ends.'

In his book, Korneyev stressed the dangers involved for Soviet Jews who maintained contact with world Jewry. Israel is evil, world Jewry is an instrument of that evil, the United States is using such forces to further its own anti-Soviet goals, and patriotic Soviet citizens must therefore beware of contamination. It is their loyalty that is at risk.

The Soviet authorities conduct a public and at times ferocious campaign against both the refuseniks and the dissidents. But refuseniks are not dissidents: they do not share the dissident dream of a radical change in the Soviet system. Held back, harassed, imprisoned, the refuseniks still cling to their hopes of an exit visa. Those who have been in prison, labour camp or exile, are particularly alert to charges of treachery, or to anti-Semitism, for they have been through a testing time, and their fate affects not only their fellow refuseniks, but all Jews who might wish to contemplate living as Jews, or applying to leave for the Jewish State.

Who is chosen for abuse or arrest, for denunciation or for trial, seems to be a lottery: a system of random action intended to create widespread fear and uncertainty. A minority are chosen for public obloquy, for verdicts of guilty. This is not inefficiency, but clever calculation: a warning to those not yet picked upon that they could just as easily be singled out, and just as ruthlessly punished.

The western visitor is amazed at the cheerfulness of the refuseniks. The authorities have refused them visas: they refuse, for their part, to give in. 'I am sure that the time will come and we shall meet again,' one of them wrote to me recently.

The Jews of Hope

The Soviet authorities have no shortage of 'reasons' for maintaining refusals. Among the versions which came to my notice were:

'Your departure is not in the interest of the Soviet Union.'

'Your emigration is considered at present to be inexpedient.'

'You are refused because you have no close relatives in Israel.'

'Let your mother return from Israel *to* the Soviet Union.'

'You'll crumble before you get out.'

'You are refused – Go away!'

The individual goes away, as ordered. But his aspirations, and his Jewishness, cannot be so easily pushed aside. An example of this was a recent course on Yiddish and Jewish ethnography, approved by the Communist Party and held in Moscow under the auspices of the 'official' Yiddish journal *Sovietishe Heimland*, a magazine often hostile to Jewish aspirations. The journal's editor, Aron Vergelis, took the chair. Two non-Jewish specialists gave papers based on documents only available with official sanction.

Being official lectures, at first only a handful of people turned up. Then news spread that here were lectures in which the word 'Jew' was being spoken in a scientific, civilized way. By the fourth seminar, more than a hundred people had enrolled. Then, without warning, the lectures were stopped.

What had gone wrong? One of those present told me how, by the fourth lecture, many of those present were refuseniks. No Hebrew was spoken, but the enthusiasm for a 'Jewish' subject was manifest. As another of the participants, a refusenik, told a friend: 'After the course had been cancelled, thirty of us tried to continue the ethnographical studies ourselves. But without the essential documentation it was not possible for us. We did, however, have a taste of how marvellous it would be, if only the authorities recognized the hunger that exists among Soviet Jews for any scrap of information about their past.'

Speaking to a third participant, I learned of just how exciting it had been for the refuseniks present to listen openly and officially to a lecture on Jewish life, albeit the scientific study of numbers, and how each of them felt a renewed sense of commitment and participation. The authorities had acted, but too late. As one of those present told me: 'The word Jew was pronounced, without creating a feeling of fear.'

Because the word Jew is often pronounced in quite another way, Jews are drawn continually closer together. 'To most Soviet citizens,' one refusenik told me, 'you are a Jew, and you are treated like a Jew. Some Jews can dissolve – they can assimilate. But for very many Jews assimilation doesn't work, so much so that sons go against their fathers, who have assimilated and are part of the system.'

This particular refusenik was the son of an assimilated father, a Communist who had risen to become Secretary of the Communist Party in his Institute. 'They were building an extension,' the son recalled. 'Father gave orders. Then he went on holiday. When he returned he found that all was not as he had wished. He summoned his deputies – they were educated people. Suddenly they turned on him and said. "You were on vacation. It's just like Jews always do. You go away. And when you come back, you make a big noise."

'Father was shattered. To be insulted *as a Jew*! He had always tried to persuade us – his two sons – that we were the fools, to be at all interested in being Jews. Now he admitted we were right. Shortly afterwards he died of a heart attack. He died as a Jew.'

9

'What will happen tomorrow?'

———◇———

Spring 1967. Moscow still has diplomatic relations with the State of Israel. An Israeli singer is billed to appear at one of the city's main concert halls. Among those who come to hear her is an engineering graduate, a Jew, aged thirty-four. Openly, he carries a tape-recorder and all the necessary apparatus. As the concert proceeds, he records the songs of Israel, sung in modern Hebrew – the language of Israel.

The young man makes the recording not for himself alone, but for the many other young Jews who wish to hear, to hear again, and to learn by heart, the songs of the Jewish State. His name is Yosif Begun. Four years later, at the age of thirty-eight, he applies for emigration to Israel.

———◇———

Soon after applying for his exit visa, Yosif Begun lost his job as an engineer, and was dismissed from the Moscow Engineering Institute where he was doing post-doctoral research. A year later, as immigration to Israel gathered momentum throughout the Soviet Union, he was among a group of refuseniks who decided to ask the authorities for permission to teach Hebrew. Such Hebrew teaching, they believed, was an important part of the preparation of Jews for immigration. Permission to teach was refused.

Without a job, and unable to continue his engineering research, Begun decided to give Hebrew lessons without permission. For five years he managed to teach Hebrew privately, unhampered by the authorities. During those years his influence as a teacher grew, and his reputation spread. Jews came to him to learn, not only their language, but also their history and culture.

On 22 January 1977 Begun was one of the four Soviet Jews singled out for personal attack in the television film *Traders of Souls*. As Begun himself explained, in a letter of protest, 'the film persistently suggests to viewers that the Jewish emigrants are not harmless people, but rather that they are betraying their true homeland and are leaving for a State which has only one goal: aggression (on the screen one sees smoke and ashes, bombing and devastation); and the main consequence of this agression is the murder of children (on the screen one sees disfigured bodies of murdered children).' According to *Traders of Souls*, those Jews in prison were not 'prisoners of conscience', but 'hooligans and speculators receiving a just punishment' for having received money from Zionist organizations, pursuing underground 'anti-Soviet activity', and meeting 'in secret places' with American Congressmen, Israeli athletes 'and other "Zionist Agents" '.

Begun's letter of protest continued: 'The film lasts for more than an hour and leaves the viewer with a deep impression. Its anti-Zionist and anti-Israeli thrust cannot hide its anti-Jewish essence. An uninformed

124

viewer gets the feeling of dislike and suspicion of all Jews. Those people who decide to emigrate, or who get a refusal and try to defend their right to leave, are therefore put in a very difficult and dangerous situation.'

Despite the television film attack, Begun continued to teach Hebrew. But at the same time he was repeatedly refused permission to register as a Hebrew teacher. Under Soviet law he was therefore unemployed, and on 3 March 1977 he was arrested. Charged with leading 'a parasitic way of life', Begun was held in prison for three months.

On 1 June 1977 Begun was brought to trial. 'Had the Hebrew language been treated like any other language,' he told the court, 'I would have been registered as a teacher of Hebrew and I would not have been in court today . . . I worked for twenty years in a remunerative job. Why on earth should I have left my job at the point when I was upgraded from a technician to a scientific worker? Do you assume that I had lost my reason? I will tell you why I lost my job. In April 1971 I submitted an application for emigration to Israel and soon afterwards I was deprived of my job.'

Begun was sentenced to two years in exile in Siberia. On his release on 5 March 1978, he returned to Moscow, the city in which he had lived for most of his life. But the housing authorities refused to grant him permission to re-register in the capital. Scarcely ten weeks after his release from Siberia, he was again arrested, and accused of violating residence regulations.

At a second trial, which was held on 28 June 1978, Begun was sentenced to three years' exile. Bernard Levin wrote in *The Times*, on 27 February 1980: 'From the moment of Begun's first application for an exit visa, he had been continually harassed. He was arrested many times, his home was repeatedly searched by KGB officers and his property stolen by them, and in the Nazi-like anti-Semitic television film *Traders of Souls*, he was, along with Anatoly Shcharansky and other victims of Soviet anti-Semitism, personally vilified.' A study of Begun's treatment, Levin wrote, 'and in particular his two "trials", reveals that there were some twenty flagrant breaches of Soviet law or the constitution on the part of the authorities . . . .'

'Throughout all this,' Levin declared, 'Yosif Begun has displayed a fortitude in adversity and a courage in resisting oppression that mark him as a truly exceptional being; to read through, as I have done, a complete collection of the appeals, protests, statements he has sent to various individuals, journals and organizations in his own country and abroad is to catch a glimpse of the best that humanity can do and be. Again and again, it is not his own case he is pleading, but that of some fellow-sufferer or his persecuted people as a whole.'

After Begun's second release, in 1981, he was again refused permission to return to his home in Moscow. Instead, he was forced to live in Strunino, a small town more than fifty miles outside the capital. This ruling effectively prevented him from continuing the Hebrew lessons which, beginning more than nine years before, he had given to an ever-widening circle.

Begun's divorced second wife Ala Drugova, and her son Boris, whom Begun had adopted, were both allowed to emigrate to Israel in November 1981.

On 20 October 1982, the authorities moved against Begun for the third time. They did so by striking at his friend, Ina Shlemova-Speranskaya, whom he hoped to marry. That day KGB agents raided Ina's small Moscow apartment and seized several tape-recorder cassettes, containing English-language lessons, Hebrew-language lessons and Hebrew songs. Also seized were a tape-recorder, a radio and a typewriter, copies of an Israeli journal, *Twenty Two*, published in Russian, back numbers of the privately printed Jewish 'underground' broadsheet of the 1970s, *Jews in the USSR*, and many private documents, including Begun's Savings Bank Book.

In all, from the small library, 112 books and pamphlets were taken, each carefully listed in the official 'receipt'. These included Ber Mark's standard history of the Warsaw ghetto uprising of 1943, Max Dimont's textbook, *Jews, God and History*, Menachem Begin's memoirs, *White Nights*, describing his days in a Soviet labour camp, a book on the Entebbe hijack rescue, and Yosif Begun's own collection of materials on Jewish culture, *Our Heritage*.

The search of Ina's apartment lasted five hours. Pressed by one of the agents to say that these papers and other materials belonged to Begun, Ina refused to do so. As the search continued, Begun himself arrived at the apartment. Both were arrested.

At first Ina refused to accompany the investigators, whose names were Burtsev and Kazaryants, to the police station. It was illegal, she pointed out, under Soviet law, for a person to be questioned in the hours of darkness. The two men put pressure on her to sign a statement that all the confiscated materials belonged to Begun, but this she categorically refused to do.

Following her refusal, Ina was taken to the police station and asked to give testimony against Begun.

Again she refused, arguing that whereas she had been informed that all the confiscated materials were being considered anti-Soviet, they were in fact quite obviously connected with Jewish culture. This, she insisted, was in no way a crime.

After five hours of questioning, Begun and Ina were released. It was a busy week for the KGB in Moscow. Four days after Begun's release, a large posse of militiamen prevented a group of Jewish chess players from entering the apartment of chess grandmaster Boris Gulko, a member of the Soviet national chess team. The chess players had wished to show their support for Gulko, who was on hunger strike in protest against the refusal of the authorities since 1979 to grant him, his wife Anna and their three-year-old son David exit visas to Israel. 'Blocking the apartment', the standard move against meetings, had once more proved effective. Gulko's hunger strike was in vain: he called it off, believing that no one in the West would be able to persuade the authorities to grant him a visa.

Yosif Begun, meanwhile, having been released from questioning, was unmolested for nearly three weeks. He and Ina went to Leningrad, to stay at a friend's apartment, to rest and regather their strength. The couple spent their last Friday evening in Leningrad with a religious Hebrew teacher and other refusenik friends: an evening in which joy and foreboding were intermingled.

On 6 November 1982 Ina and Yosif left their friend's apartment for the Moscow railway station, and for the day train to Moscow. As they were boarding the train, KGB agents were waiting for them. They were taken off, and with them some books which Begun had in a bag:

books on Jewish history, and on the Hebrew language, with which, as it were, he had been caught 'red-handed'. He was, of course, making no attempt to conceal them.

Begun was held in custody, and questioned, for twenty-two hours without a break. Then he was taken to Vladimir prison, a hundred miles east of Moscow. Distraught, Ina demanded to know his alleged crime. She was given no answer.

Begun remained in prison, still without any charge being made against him, and was refused permission to receive any visitors. Ina and the twenty-year-old son Borukh, Begun's son by his first marriage, had their repeated requests to visit him turned down.

As Ina told me this story, she produced with pride a charming snapshot of Begun and his son on holiday by the banks of a river not far from Moscow. Begun's face was wreathed in smiles, as he and his son enjoyed the precious moments of relaxation. Unfortunately, this photograph was one of those taken away from me by customs officials at Moscow airport.

Following Begun's imprisonment at Vladimir in November 1982, the authorities began to build up their case against him. Rumours soon spread among his many Jewish friends that he would face charges under the notorious Article 70 of the Russian Soviet Socialist Republic's Criminal Code, concerning anti-Soviet agitation and propaganda. This Article contains one of the most serious charges that a refusenik can face, far more serious than Begun's two earlier charges, for which he was given a two-year and a three-year sentence respectively.

Article 70 specifies 'agitation or propaganda' carried on for the purpose 'of subverting or weakening the

The Jews of Hope

Soviet regime or of committing particular, especially dangerous crimes against the State', or the circulation, preparation or 'keeping' of literature for the purpose 'of slanderous fabrications which defame the Soviet State and social system'.

Many refuseniks know the principal Articles of the Criminal Code by heart, or can in a moment find the relevant volume on their bookshelves. The realization that Begun was being considered as a case for Article 70 struck a chill of fear, for him as its victim, and for all refuseniks for whom this case was clearly intended as a warning and a deterrent.

Begun's friends in the Soviet Union and abroad were not idle. In the first month after his arrest a dossier of his case was drawn up and submitted to all western delegates at the Madrid Conference on Human Rights. Two months later, on 13 January 1983, Ina was allowed to visit Vladimir prison for the first time, and to hand over to the authorities there a five-kilogramme food parcel for Begun. But she was not allowed to see him, and when she asked for details of the charge that had been prepared against him, she was given no clear answer.

Returning to Moscow, Ina sought the services of a defence lawyer. But none of the lawyers whom she approached was willing to take up Begun's case. 'Once they become aware that the KGB is actively engaged with investigations,' she told a friend, 'one lawyer after another withdraws.' This was after Begun had been held in Vladimir prison for eighty-three days, without anyone being allowed to see him, or to communicate with him.

Ina Shlemova, a woman in her forties, is not easily

browbeaten. Despite the constant supervision of her own apartment, and the obviously serious nature of Begun's case, she had already taken up cudgels on his behalf. On 10 January 1983 she wrote to the Procurator of the Vladimir Region, Mr Tsarev, and to the Procurator of the Russian Soviet Socialist Republic, Mr Kravtsov, to protest against Begun's imprisonment.

On 1 February 1983 Ina was summoned by the KGB for 'investigation'. While she was being questioned at the KGB headquarters in central Moscow, by Constantine Zotov, then head of the KGB's Jewish section, another KGB officer entered her apartment and began to question her seventy-five-year-old mother. This questioning continued for five hours.

Ina refused to be cowed, or to abandon her Yosif to oblivion. Early in February she wrote once more to Tsarev and Kravtsov. In the course of her letter she asked: 'What kind of crime did my husband commit causing the authorities to try to prove his guilt using methods which offend human dignity and which undermine faith in the Soviet legal system? Three months have elapsed since the day my husband was arrested, and I still have had no official notification of the Article under which he is being charged.'

On 10 February 1983 Tsarev replied that Begun might indeed be accused of 'criminal responsibility' for 'activity covered by Article 70' of the Russian Republic's Criminal Code. Ina replied six days later, her letter setting out Begun's defence in clear courageous terms. 'It would be a natural and humanitarian act', she ended, 'if instead of organizing a legal process against him, you will permit Yosif Begun and his family to emigrate to Israel.'

131

The Jews of Hope

On the last day of February Ina was warned by the authorities: 'No more noise from abroad.' This warning, made to so many refuseniks, serves only to encourage them. The warning itself is proof for them that 'noise' on their behalf does affect the authorities. Such warnings also indicate to the refusenik that there is indeed some form of protest afoot in the West on their behalf, that they are not forgotten, and that the authorities are fully aware of the extent to which outsiders are concerned about the daily plight of Soviet Jews.

On 1 March 1983 refuseniks in Moscow and Leningrad went on hunger strike on Begun's behalf. I myself was in Moscow that day, and heard many Jews speak of his kindness, his love of learning, his abilities as a teacher, his charm and his courage. In Ina's words two days later, as we sat at a secluded table in a small suburban restaurant, sheltered by the blare of pop music: 'They thought they would punish Yosif without so many people being concerned. They didn't think so many people would care. They told him, "Nobody will know about you." '

Ina wears on her wrist a bracelet engraved with the date of Begun's second arrest, 17 May 1978. She speaks of her hopes that one day she and Yosif may be allowed to go to Israel. As she speaks, a new record bursts out over the restaurant's loudspeakers. It is the Abba song, 'I have a dream', and while Ina herself speaks of the dream of Jerusalem, words which she does not understand reflect her own mood of hope amid hopelessness: 'When I know the time is ripe for me, I'll cross the street. I have a dream . . . .'

We leave the restaurant, and return across Moscow to Ina's apartment, shadowed all the while by a KGB agent, her 'tail'. Once settled in her small drawing room, and with a glance out of the window at the KGB car parked below, Ina speaks about Begun's personal history, and his struggle. 'His grandfather was a rabbi in White Russia. His father died when he was a little boy. Many of his relatives were killed in the Second World War.' As for Begun himself, she says, 'he has committed no crime. He is not a criminal. All he wants is to go to Israel.'

Ina speaks of her last visit to Vladimir, a week earlier. Although still not allowed to see Begun, she had been handed a letter in which he expressed his worries about Ina herself, and about his son Borukh. Re-reading the letter, Ina comments: 'Borukh is a brave boy and he loves his father. But he is only a boy. He needs his student's life.'

The pressures which the authorities can put on the son of a refusenik are considerable. There is the constant threat of an end of his studies. There are the continual petty harassments by fellow students, encouraged to be abusive, to poison the character of a father in front of his son; in front of a vulnerable and lonely boy who must submit to such abuse, who must listen to such poison, day in and day out, if the authorities will it.

As Ina thinks about Borukh and the troubles to which he may be subjected at any time, she 'defends' Begun's work and character, his Hebrew-language lessons and his study groups on Jewish culture. 'His work is important', she says, 'for Jews who know nothing about their history.' Like Begun himself, Ina is convinced that material about Jewish history, about Jewish culture, and about anti-Semitism, needs to be taught, 'especially' as she expresses it, 'at this period of time, just now'.

We sit at Begun's own desk, surrounded by the remnant of his books – those that were not seized during the raid four months ago. The room has an air of expectancy about it, as if Begun himself might walk in at any moment, and renew his studies, or even his teaching. The force of his character is in the room, a brooding, but also a vibrant, presence. Ina is talking again about Begun's teaching. 'He is an enlightener by nature,' she says. 'Many people love him, whom he teaches.'

Begun has asked Ina to send him, to prison, a parcel of books and materials, including dictionaries, to enable him to study both Yiddish and German. 'Hurrying to master more and more subjects,' she explains, 'Yosif only allows himself five hours a night for sleeping. He is hungry for many subjects.'

Darkness falls. Outside the entrance to the apartment block a KGB agent waits and watches. Ina and her mother are alone. 'What will happen tomorrow?' Ina asks. Then, as if in answer to her own question, she tells me: 'I don't know what will happen tomorrow.'

———◇———

On 15 March 1983 Ina went once more by train to Vladimir, to hand over the statutory five-kilogramme parcel. She was allowed to include a packet of 'mazzot' – unleavened bread for Passover. But two books Begun had asked for – a Russian-Hebrew dictionary and a Yiddish study book – were not accepted. Nine days later, when Ina telephoned the office of the Investigator, she was told that the investigation was not yet completed, so that there was 'no point' in her looking for a defence lawyer.

'What will happen tomorrow?'

Within a month, on 11 April 1983, Ina was asked to return to Vladimir prison. Once more she took the train eastward. She was now told that the investigation had been concluded, and that Begun would definitely be tried under Article 70. She was shaken, even terrified, by what that meant: a possible sentence of up to twelve years, the first seven years to be served in prison, followed by five years in exile.

While she was at Vladimir, Ina, although still not allowed to see Begun, was shown a note which he had written for her. But she was only allowed to read a single line of it, in which he authorized her to engage a lawyer on his behalf. The rest of the letter was deliberately covered over by the officials present.

Engaging a lawyer was not easy. Ina was told that she could choose only from the Vladimir panel of thirty lawyers, of whom twenty-six were not allowed to participate in what are called 'security cases'. Of the remainder, three indicated that they were unwilling or unable to represent Begun. Notwithstanding this, Ina was required to find somebody within a week, so that on 18 April 1983 Begun himself and a lawyer could consider the case that was being brought against him.

Friends of the couple reported in the first week of April that although Ina had hitherto shown exemplary courage in her dealings both with the KGB and with the prison authorities, she was in tears at the task now facing her and her Yosif.

At the end of April a lawyer was found who was willing to act for Begun. His name was Leonid Maksimovich Popov. At the end of April 1983 Popov saw Begun for several hours, and discussed the nature of Begun's defence. Popov agreed with Begun that all the material confiscated from Ina's apartment 'could only be described as Hebrew study material' and that, in his view as a lawyer, nothing in Begun's actions fell within the category of criminal intent.

Popov reported all this to Ina on 4 May 1983. But he also told her that, her efforts to have herself officially registered as Begun's wife having failed, she would almost certainly be summoned as a witness for the prosecution. Refusal to give witness against Begun could result in a heavy prison sentence for Ina herself. Meanwhile, Popov added, Begun was taking an active, and indeed 'meticulous' part in the preparation of his defence. Too much so, it soon appeared, for Popov withdrew from the case during June, leaving Begun to complete his own defence.

As an observant Jew, Begun was unwilling to work on his defence during the Sabbath. But that was the day on which the prison authorities deliberately chose to bring him essential documents. Refusing to read them, he left the room. But he was then brought back in handcuffs and forced to listen while the documents were read to him.

At his trial Begun will argue that the teaching of Jewish culture is as legal as the teaching of any national culture inside the Soviet Union. He will assert that, of all the Soviet nationalities enjoying cultural rights by law, only the Jews are denied these rights in reality. He will cite two non-Jewish writers, both members of Soviet minorities, who have, in official books, expounded the cultural rights of their respective nationalities. One of these writers, Raul Gamzatov, wrote in the obscure Avarian language of the Caucasian region of Dagestan. The other, Yury Richteu, wrote in the equally obscure

Chukchi language of the Soviet far north. Both these authors have been officially acclaimed by the Soviet Press for their discovery and revival of neglected languages. Begun will assert that Hebrew, the language of the Jews, is no less real as a language, and no less an essential part of the nationality 'Jew' in his internal passport, and in the internal passports of more than two million other 'Soviet citizens of Jewish nationality': their official Soviet designation.

Ought Begun to assert so forcefully, and with such conviction, the rights which he believes each Soviet Jew possesses? Ought he to have gone on trying to teach his fellow Jews something of their historical, cultural and linguistic heritage, despite so many warnings, despite so much punishment? Ought he to have risked a third, and probably far more savage, sentence? These questions several of his friends discussed with me in Moscow and in Leningrad. 'Yosif is a non-realist,' said one. 'He behaves too tough. He will not compromise.' Yet such critical comments were made by men and women who will themselves unhesitatingly defend Begun's right to teach, and will do everything they can, against all obstacles, to carry forward the torch he has lit. The fear is that he will receive a savage sentence in order to deter them.

On 6 July 1983, less than three weeks before the date was set for Begun's trial, Ina Shlemova once more took the train to Vladimir. There she met the prison Commandant, Zagumenikov, who told her that Begun would not be allowed to have his monthly parcel, due on 14 July, nor would he be permitted to buy food in the prison kiosk with his monthly allowance, as he had 'broken the regulations' while doing exercises during his daily walk. During the walk, in the sweltering heat, he had taken off his shirt. It was this which was forbidden.

During her visit on 6 July, Ina was neither allowed to see Begun nor to send him a letter.

———◇———

July, August and September passed without a trial. Begun remained in Vladimir prison. In London, the House of Commons All-Party Committee for Soviet Jewry gave him its annual award; it was accepted for him by Benjamin Fain, Begun's friend, now a Professor in Israel. East of Vladimir, at another prison, Anatoly Shcharansky reached, on 15 September 1983, the point in his thirteen year sentence when remission, and indeed early release, became technically possible. But despite a continuing campaign in the West, and his wife Avital's unrelenting efforts on his behalf, he remained in prison.

Ina Shlemova in Moscow, Avital Shcharansky in Jerusalem, struggle against a regime which is unmoved by a wife's anguish, or by the loyalty of separation and adversity. 'Well, it's our life,' reflects Evgeni Lein, 'and we must struggle for freedom.'

Lein had been with Begun a few hours before Begun's arrest. Together they had walked the streets of Leningrad, stopping only to drink a glass of tea. Now, each time Lein drinks tea, he remembers that Begun will be without it – 'I had only warm water instead of tea in prison.' Lein also remembers how Begun had sensed that he would be arrested. 'He spoke about it calmly and with self-respect.'

On 14 October 1983, Yosif Begun, at the age of fifty-one, was given the maximum sentence, seven years in prison to be followed by five years in exile.

10

'A strong spirit'

———◇———

Irina Brailovsky is forty-seven years old. With her husband Victor, she first applied for an exit visa more than ten years ago, in 1972. Her husband was then a lecturer in probability theory and mathematical statistics at the Moscow Radio Technical Institute. Irina was a mathematician working with computers. As is almost always the case, the moment of application was also the moment of dismissal: Victor Brailovsky was sacked from his Institute, and Irina from her job at the Moscow Computing Centre.

Up to the time of their application for a visa, both Victor and Irina had published many scientific articles. Since applying, neither has been allowed to publish. At one point Victor was told that he could leave the Soviet Union, but would have to go without Irina and their children, Leonid and Dalia. He refused.

After waiting in vain for a visa for four years, Victor Brailovsky embarked upon a seventeen-day hunger strike. It was to no avail. Since his hunger strike, however, he has suffered from a serious liver condition. His father and his brother Michael were both given permission to leave the Soviet Union. Today they live in

Israel. But Victor and his family were refused permission to join them.

Shortly after his first application to go to Israel had been refused, Victor Brailovsky became involved in a cyclostyled publication, *Jews in the USSR*. This entirely unofficial journal sought, in a series of articles, to examine the Jewish problem in the Soviet Union. The first two issues were published in 1972. Throughout the period of publication the names of successive editors, and of the authors of the articles, were printed in the journal. Despite the outspoken nature of many of the articles, publication continued for more than seven years. In all, twenty issues were compiled and circulated.

The authorities took no action against *Jews in the USSR*. Indeed, many of those who wrote articles in the journal, as well as several of the editors, were subsequently given permission to emigrate to Israel. Since they had no wish to be martyrs, but only emigrants, all the writers, including Brailovsky, took care that their articles were within the law.

Several of the articles in *Jews in the USSR* gave details of the discrimination against Soviet Jews in general, and against those who applied for visas in particular. Other articles examined distortions in the writing of Jewish history in Soviet books and newspapers. An article by Brailovsky himself gave details of numerous historical distortions in the Soviet press, including the justification of Tsarist pogroms, and the denigration of Zionism by use of falsehoods.

As a result of having been denied the possibility of continuing, officially, with his scientific work, Brailovsky had also joined with a number of other Soviet Jews to organize a small private scientific seminar. Its subject was the scientific topic, Collective Phenomena, and after a while the meetings were held in the Brailovskys' own cramped apartment. In 1974 the scientists involved decided to hold a special international session of their seminar, and to invite scientists from abroad. In an attempt to stop this international seminar, Brailovsky and the other organizers were arrested, and held in prison for fifteen days. These were the very days when the seminar was to have taken place. The seminar had to be abandoned.

Undeterred, Brailovsky began to collect material for a special 'Symposium of Jewish Culture'. In December 1976 his apartment was searched, and much of his material confiscated. Meanwhile, the scientific seminar continued to meet, and further international sessions were planned. The searches of Brailovsky's small apartment became regular occurrences, as did the confiscation of his material. But the seminar continued, and in December 1978 the confidently named Third International Conference on Collective Phenomena was held in the Brailovsky apartment. It lasted for three days. Among those who presented scientific papers were Brailovsky himself, his wife Irina, and several leading United States, British, Swiss, French and Soviet Jewish scientists. The proceedings of the conference were subsequently published by the New York Academy of Sciences.

In April 1980 a fourth international conference was planned, also to be held in the Brailovsky apartment. Three days before it was due to begin, the police broke down the Brailovskys' door, ransacked the apartment, confiscated a mass of scientific papers, and took

Brailovsky away for interrogation. After five hours he was released with a warning not to allow the conference to take place. He ignored the warning.

The Fourth International Conference on Collective Phenomena was duly held. Seven months later, on 13 November 1980, Brailovsky was arrested. No charges were made, no reasons given for his arrest. He was kept in prison for seven months without trial.

Amid international protest, Brailovsky's case was taken up by the British writer Bernard Levin, who, a year earlier, had publicized Yosif Begun's plight. On 15 January 1981, two months after Brailovsky's arrest, Levin urged Russian-speaking readers of *The Times* to telephone the Chief Moscow Investigator, Georgyi Ponomarev, or his deputy, Smirnov, to ask the reasons for Brailovsky's imprisonment, and the nature of the charges to be made against him. Levin gave the telephone numbers of the two officials.

In his concluding paragraph, Levin wrote: 'The persecution of Dr Brailovsky is a scandal that ought to unite the entire body of western science in a plain statement that unless he is freed and allowed to leave the Soviet Union with his wife and children, scientific exchanges will be suspended. Only such an action can save him; if it is not taken, the Soviet Union will have scored a notable victory, every Soviet scientist who has contemplated either emigration or speaking up for civil rights will begin to think better of it, and science herself will have been betrayed.'

As far as the Soviet authorities were concerned, two 'threats' converged in Brailovsky: that he was the leader of an unofficial but significant scientific seminar and that he was also a leader in a growing cultural and national movement. The seminar had obtained world publicity. But to strike at Brailovsky, and at the strength which he represented, the authorities decided to use the defunct journal, *Jews in the USSR*, which was to form the sole basis of the charge against him. The journal had ceased publication two years before, in the summer of 1979. At no time during the seven years in which it had been produced had Brailovsky, or any of the others responsible for its publication been told to cease publication. The only warnings Brailovsky had received, and they were many, had been to give up the scientific seminar, and to cancel the international conferences. This he had always refused to do.

In *Jews in the USSR*, Brailovsky and his fellow writers had drawn attention on several occasions to anti-Semitic publications in the Soviet Union. They had given details of anti-Jewish discrimination, and explained something of the difficulties and disabilities put in the way of Jews who sought to emigrate to Israel. The charge against him now alleged that, in the years 1973 to 1980, he had 'systematically engaged in the preparation and distribution in written, typewritten and other forms of material containing deliberately false fabrications defaming the Soviet regime and the Soviet social system'.

The trial was held in Moscow on 18 July 1981. Brailovsky defended himself against the charges item by item. He had been accused of defaming the Soviet system by stating that Jews who intend to emigrate to Israel were 'victims of the arbitrariness of the administration'.

'I do not have precise statistics,' he told the court, 'but to make up for that, I know only too well the sad experiences of my own family and many others. After

143

submitting an application for exit permits in 1972, I was dismissed from work, my wife Irina was forced to leave her job, and we fell into the category of refuseniks. Since 1975 the authorities have told us that the reason for our refusal is my wife's involvement in secret work. However, in 1978, after a special inquiry, the leadership of Moscow University – the only organization for which she had worked – declared that Irina had actually never been engaged in secret work and that Moscow University had no objection to her leaving the country. The Rector of Moscow University, Academician Logunov, made this declaration not only to Irina personally but also to a number of foreign scholars. Nevertheless, at the same time, the leadership of the USSR Ministry of the Interior continued to repeat its refusal. In particular, this was done by Deputy-Minister of the Interior Shumilin. And so for many years the desire of my family to be reunited with our close relatives – my father and brother – has remained unrealized.'

During Brailovsky's trial the Soviet State sought to challenge, and to deny, four specific charges made in *Jews in the USSR*. These charges had been made four, five and even six years earlier, but no action taken against them then. They were, first, that Jews in the Soviet Union were discriminated against in culture and education; second, that anti-Semitism was a feature of current Soviet society; third, that the Jewish religion was being denigrated; and, fourth, that unfair restrictions were being placed on Jewish emigration. This was the first trial in which the situation of the Jews themselves, rather than some imaginary issue of treachery or hooliganism or parasitism, was the central theme.

Brailovsky understood that it was the truth about the

situation of Soviet Jewry that the court sought to deny. In the course of his defence he gave a detailed survey of the harsh situation confronting the Jews of modern Russia.

Brailovsky was found guilty and sentenced to five years in exile. He was sent to a remote village in the Soviet Republic of Kazakhstan, not far from the Caspian Sea. Irina is allowed to visit him there, and indeed to live with him. To do so, however, she must leave her son and daughter for long periods. At the time of the trial her son Leonid was nineteen, her daughter Dalia, six.

In the last week of June 1982 Brailovsky received a favourable *karakteristika*, or character reference, from his workplace in exile, stating that he was 'a good worker, behaves correctly and also fulfils his social duties'.

Such favourable references are extremely rare for Soviet political prisoners. Brailovsky was even told by the foreman of his work gang that, on the basis of this favourable reference, there might be a possibility of his trying to obtain an early release, under Article 53 of the Criminal Code of the Russian Republic.

Brailovsky's foreman promised to do what he could to bring the matter to the notice of the appropriate authorities. But later, when Brailovsky asked where the matter stood, the foreman became evasive, and two months later, at the end of August 1982, Brailovsky was reprimanded for 'missing a half day's work'. He had told the foreman he was not feeling well, and had received the foreman's permission to be absent. But clearly the matter had reached those 'highest authorities' who did not wish Brailovsky to obtain an early release. His wife now fears that he will have to serve his full term.

Irina Brailovsky is a scientist in her own right. Her

contribution to the scientific seminars was of the highest quality. She is also a woman of courage. To a visitor from Britain who was worried about the possible danger involved in visiting refuseniks she remarked: 'Don't be so afraid. It is no crime.'

Thirty years ago Irina Brailovsky, then aged seventeen, had gone with Victor to the Lenin Library in Moscow, to ask to read the Bible. They were told, 'It is closed.' 'Why?' they asked. 'It is religious propaganda,' was the reply.

The Brailovskys were never deterred by such obstacles. From that very moment, as Irina explained when I visited her in Moscow, 'the possibility of going to Israel inspired us – not to change the system here, but to *ask* to leave. The more we were suppressed and crushed, the more we resisted.'

Irina is under no illusions about the results of the severity of current Soviet policy: 'Now people are much less active than they were before,' she explains. 'They are much more fearful. They are much more submitted to fear than three years ago.' Such new fears are inevitable, she believes, 'with the closing of emigration'. Irina refuses, however, to give way to pessimism. 'Given the Jewish fate,' she says, 'people cannot allow themselves *not* to be optimists. They cannot dare, in their horrible fate, not to be optimists – to survive. They cannot afford the luxury of being pessimists.'

Irina is neither a pessimist nor a defeatist. She will fight on, for her husband, for her children, for her right to go to Israel, for the right of all Soviet Jews to leave, should they wish to do so. The example of her determination is widely felt. As one leading refusenik told me, 'Under great pressure, when her husband had been arrested, Irina went on. Her daughter was ill, her mother ill, her husband in prison. In this situation she was acting like a strong spirit, very strong. She is not a soft reasoning person. She has a bursting temperament. But there is always reasoning behind it. She is always explaining her views. I respect her very much.'

'When I feel something weak inside *me*,' this same refusenik commented, 'I want to spend twenty minutes with *her*. She is a woman with balls – and with brains. I followed her advice when *I* had doubts, fears.'

———◇———

Irina Brailovsky's character inspires not only her fellow Soviet Jews. I, too, sitting in her small apartment, feel the strength of her character. From her window we can see the Olympic village, built for the Moscow Olympics of 1980. My companion, Jonathan Wootliff, mentions to Irina the decision of the Student Committee for Soviet Jewry in Britain not to use the 1980 Olympics as a forum for public protest. Irina is indignant. 'Why did nobody come out?' she asks. 'It was very much put across that the visitors were just puppets: in their hotels, at the circus or the ballet, at the Games themselves. Nothing was done to ask the authorities about us on that occasion. It would have been very difficult,' Irina comments, 'for the Soviet officials to have handled all this crowd of people. They would not have been able to handle them. You would not have been submitted to punishment.'

Beneath a photograph of Theodor Herzl and a drawing of Albert Einstein, Irina insists that the Olympics were a particularly opportune moment for public protest in Moscow itself. 'Why', she asks, 'didn't you Western people – who were quite unpunishable – why didn't you come and – in a dignified way – *ask* about us?'

To Wootliff's reply that after 'careful consideration' in London it had been decided not to make any protest in Moscow itself, Irina comments, 'It was a wrong decision. Your task is to help us in our rather horrible fate. You enabled them to use you as their own puppets. They cannot cut off contact. They need your visits much more than you do. After your behaviour at the Olympics it was much easier for them to handle tourists as they wished. It is their propaganda that diminishes your involvement in our case. They gave the impression that you cannot come, or cannot make contact. It is not so.'

To the argument that western activity would not have been effective, Irina replies: 'Your behaviour, your decision not to make protests here during the Olympics, this showed the officials here that western support could be very easily handled. It is the existence of the concern of the western world that stops them', she pauses, 'hanging all of us.'

Irina falls silent. We seek to assure her that western protests will not flag. She disappears into the kitchen, returning a few moments later with a pot of tea, an even larger pot of boiling water, bread, butter and biscuits. We ask if her daughter Dalia will join us. But Dalia is in bed suffering from a severe cold. Or so it is thought. The symptoms of this 'cold' had first emerged during a visit to her father in Kazakhstan in June 1982. During that visit her temperature had risen well above normal, her pulse and respiration had both increased, and there was a sudden redness and puffiness of her skin, accompanied by considerable perspiration. My visit coincides with her sixth such attack.

Irina, who also looks after her sick mother, fears that these attacks, followed as they are by exhaustion and weakness, may stem from nervous tension. She is worried that Dalia's future visits to her father in Kazakhstan may precipitate further attacks. The possibility that a common cold may also bring on an attack causes Irina added concern.

Over cups of tea, Irina criticizes the view that a dialogue is possible with the Soviet authorities on western terms. 'You are just not on the true surface,' she replies. 'You are discussing on the surface of morals, of good or bad qualities of a person. Here, it is another plane altogether. The leaders here, they are not bad. Maybe they are better than your leaders. They are just different. Their rules and structures are quite out of the structures you have. It is just another kind of system.'

Irina is convinced that the Soviet authorities are sensitive to western protests, and that any 'bargain' will only come about because of that sensitivity, and in order to lessen the 'noise'. The fact that the authorities are sensitive to western noise is demonstrated, she says, in their recent admonition to a refusenik, 'Please help us to stop the noise.'

Irina Brailovsky is about to set off once more, alone, for Kazakhstan. As we say goodbye, she gives me a charming photograph of Victor outside his hut, standing with his son. This was another of the photographs taken from me at Moscow airport. But I cannot forget the sad yet hopeful eyes of the exile, so far from his aspirations, yet convinced that his day will come, and buoyed up in that conviction by his wife.

'See you in a better place,' are Irina's last words.

11

'Help me to realize my dream'

In July 1983 there were sixteen Soviet Jews in prison, labour camp or exile. Most of them had been leaders in the Jewish emigration movement, or in the teaching of Jewish culture. One of these 'Prisoners of Zion', Anatoly Shcharansky, had been sentenced in July 1978 to thirteen years' 'deprivation of freedom'. Shcharansky's sentence and imprisonment had been a severe blow for the emigration movement, and a warning to other activists to desist. But just as Shcharansky himself, in prison, refused to give way to despair, those among whom his presence had been such an inspiration were likewise unbowed.

Shcharansky and the other fifteen 'Prisoners of Zion' pay a terrible penalty for leadership, courage and determination. At the same time, twelve former prisoners, including Shcharansky's friend Vladimir Slepak, and the woman who had helped other prisoners to maintain their morale, Ida Nudel, were still refused exit visas, despite the fact they had already served their sentences, and been released.

Although the sixteen 'Prisoners of Zion' have lost all links with Ida Nudel, they are not forgotten by those in whose cause they suffer. Many of the Jews whom I met in the Soviet Union spoke of 'the Prisoners' with deep concern. The youngest of these 'Prisoners of Zion', Simon Shnirman, was sentenced in February 1983 – two weeks before my visit – to three years in labour camp for 'draft evasion'. This was his second labour camp sentence for the same offence.

During my visit to Leningrad I met a number of his friends, and learned something of his situation. According to Soviet law, Shnirman was not eligible for service in the Red Army, being an only child, and having to look after his mother Faina, an invalid. His father David, who had fought heroically in the Soviet Navy during the Second World War, first applied to go to Israel with his family in 1959, when Simon was one year old. David was eventually allowed out, with his daughter Emma, in December 1976. Simon was refused permission to leave with his father on the grounds that he had not yet worked long enough after completing his education. David Shnirman was told, however, that his son would be allowed to leave eventually; and Simon's mother decided to stay in the Soviet Union until her son was given permission to leave.

Simon Shnirman was then working in a steel factory at Zaporozhe, an eight-hour journey from his home. When his call-up came, he saw it as a deliberate attempt by the authorities to go back on their promise to give him a visa at the same time as his mother.

Simon Shnirman was aware that if he were to do his military service, this 'conscription weapon', as it is called, could be used against him by the Soviet authorities on the grounds that he must wait between five and ten years after demobilization in order not to be

151

a 'security risk'. In 1978 he therefore informed the authorities of his refusal to serve. He was arrested, charged with draft evasion, and sentenced to two years in prison.

On 29 November 1980, after serving thirty months in a labour camp, Shnirman was released early for 'good behaviour'. He returned to his home in the Crimean town of Kerch, married, and applied at once for emigration to Israel. His grounds for applying were 'first degree kinship' with his father. His application was refused. Then, to his amazement, he was summoned once more for military service. Determined to refuse yet again, he visited his friends in Leningrad, to urge them to protest on his behalf. 'He wants noise,' I was told, 'even if the effect is bad. If there is a big noise, a little noise or no noise, it will be the same for him physically. But for his moral situation it is better, and for his wife.'

Shnirman returned to Kerch, and on 10 January 1983 he was arrested again. It was the first time that a young refusenik had been arrested on a charge of evading conscription after having already served his sentence. Simon was then twenty-five years old. His wife Elizaveta was expecting a baby. On the day before his trial was due to take place, he asked for a single day's postponement in order to prepare his defence. His mother and his wife had chosen a lawyer to defend him, but, after pressure from the authorities, the lawyer had declined to take part. His request for a postponement was refused. The trial was to take place as planned.

When Shnirman was led into court he was in handcuffs. As the trial began, in great agitation, he lacerated his wrists on the handcuffs, frustrated that he could not express himself. The trial was postponed, and

'Help me to realize my dream'

Shnirman was taken to hospital. The trial eventually took place on 14 February 1983. Once again, Shnirman appeared in court in handcuffs. He was sentenced to three years' hard labour. The court rejected his mother's plea that Soviet law grants exemption to an only son whose mother lives alone. A few weeks later, as Shnirman began his sentence, his child was born, a baby daughter named Yana.

———◇———

Even without prison, labour camp or exile, the authorities are able to make life difficult for the refuseniks. While visiting a Jewish family in Moscow I was introduced to a young man recently divorced. A year ago he applied for a visa. It was refused on the grounds that his former wife did not wish him to go. Immediately after he had been refused his visa, his wife announced that he could no longer see their four-year-old son, even for brief visits at long intervals. The young man brought a case in the courts, appealing for the right of access. His wife brought a counter-case, asking for the father to have no access at all. The court upheld the wife's plea. The young man was at once barred from seeing his son. His alimony payments had, of course, to continue.

'It's ugly,' commented one of those, himself a refusenik, hearing this story for the first time. 'Now they want to make boundaries between "loyal" Jews and "non-loyal". A "loyal Jew" can get custody of a son from a father, *and* all the advantages of a divorced wife.'

The refusal of access was not the end of the young man's troubles. The local paper – he is from a small provincial town – attacked him by name for being 'a bad man and a bad father'. His crime: wanting to go abroad and leave his son. Such articles are not published by accident, but to reflect official policy. On the basis of such an article, the Prosecutor can begin a trial.

The young man cannot receive a visa unless his former wife will agree in writing. So now he must seek to persuade her, and she, realizing how much he wants to leave, has indicated that she is persuadable, for money. The sum of money she has mentioned is so high, however, that he cannot hope to accumulate it for many years. Still, it is his *only* hope. Even with her permission finally secured, the authorities may still say 'no'.

The young man's chances of a visa are slim. He has married again, but his new wife's family are themselves refuseniks, and have been so for more than three years. 'There are those who suffer in every city,' one refusenik comments, and he goes on to tell me of another such sufferer, Victor Barshevski from Kharkov. As a young boy in the war, Barshevski was separated from his mother at the time of the German occupation of Kharkov. Taken to an orphanage, he was later looked after by another family. He never saw his mother again. She, believing him to be dead, made her way after the war to Israel: a survivor of the Kharkov massacres in which tens of thousands of Jews were murdered. Today she lives in the small town of Kvar Saba, not far from Tel Aviv.

For many years Victor Barshevski believed that his mother had been murdered by the Nazis. But in the summer of 1979 he learned that his mother was alive. He at once asked the Visa Office in Kharkov for permission to join her. Permission was refused. It has since been refused four times.

'Help me to realize my dream'

It is now more than forty years since Victor's mother last saw him; since she last held her son in her arms.

———◇———

I have told the stories of certain individual refuseniks and their families. It would need several hundred books, each larger than this one, to tell all their stories, even in outline. But it is not only the future of individuals that is endangered today, but of the whole emigration movement. Anatoly Shcharansky did not go to prison for himself alone. Ida Nudel, Vladimir Slepak and Victor Brailovsky did not risk, and find, prison and exile, in search of mere personal advantage.

Several of those to whom I spoke were afraid that the Soviet authorities might take advantage of the publicity on so few individuals by letting one or two go, even by letting Shcharansky go, in order to distract western attention from the wider problem. If Shcharansky were to be released, so the fear goes, then it might be felt in the West that the Soviet Union is loosening its grip on Soviet Jewry. But that grip might remain as tight, even tighter than today.

Western observers, and western visitors to the Soviet Union, see the extent of the refusenik problem, and the wider Jewish problem behind it. The Soviet authorities, however, deny that any such problem exists. Hence there seems no basis for any 'deal' or 'settlement'. Soviet propaganda asserts the contentment of the Jews of the Soviet Union, their wide participation in Soviet society, and their access to whatever cultural life they wish. These assertions are not borne out by the facts.

Not deals in secret, but public protests – this seems to most refuseniks to be their only hope of an eventual exit visa. Again and again I was told by refuseniks that the greater the noise from the West, the greater the chance of success: that the silence of the West would mean the end of hope. 'But for western action,' one leading refusenik commented, 'I think not only Shcharansky would have been in the dock during his trial in 1978, but many more people.' 'In the case of my husband,' another refusenik told me, 'western protest led to a lessening of the degree of his punishment.' 'It is not only for those who are punished that protest is important,' she added, 'but for the safety of others.'

Evgeni Lein, so recently returned from Siberia, told me: 'I am sure that publicity is good. Some refuseniks sit down in their apartments like a mouse. I asked for a visa louder, and I want everyone who meets me to say louder that I cannot get permission to go. As far as my visa was concerned, I was in prison in vain.' But Lein is convinced, as he expressed it, 'that if I was afraid, they would find it easier to make things difficult for me, than if I will be strong'.

I also heard worried voices that western interest might falter.

Each refusenik survives in his own way, seeking to come to terms with his or her isolation from Soviet society, and with the long wait for a visa that may never come; for a visa that has not come, in so many cases, for more than ten years. Families share the ideal of emigration, and young children grow up 'in refusal', knowing no other status. In Moscow I met a fourteen-year-old boy who told his parents five years ago, when he was only nine: 'People should be with their people.' In the following year, his parents made their first application to leave for Israel. It was rejected.

'Help me to realize my dream'

Denied the possibility of leaving, this boy's father and mother maintained their morale, first by learning Hebrew, and then by teaching it. They are teaching it still. The boy's father has frequently been threatened, harassed and, recently, imprisoned. But his spirit is unbroken.

———◇———

On my last day in Moscow, I was present at a small, private gathering of historians and writers, all but one of them refuseniks. There, I found myself talking to a young historian, who, together with his wife and mother-in-law, had been refused permission to leave. His mother-in-law's name is Bertha. This is her story.

Bertha Sokolovskaya was born in the Polish town of Bialystok on 15 December 1921. Before the First World War it had been a part of the Tsarist Empire, and Bertha's father, Efraim, had been born under Tsarist rule. At the time of her birth he was the manager of a small dyeing factory. When Bertha was four, he died. Her mother married again.

As a teenager in inter-war Poland, Bertha studied at the State Commercial Lyceum in Bialystok. Two of her best friends at the Lyceum were Lucy Albeck, who was later killed in her apartment by the Nazis, and Inna Galay, who perished in the German concentration camp of Majdanek.

Two of Bertha's cousins, Lena Fisher and Fannie Parasol, had left Poland for Palestine shortly before the outbreak of war. She has not heard of them, or from them, since. In 1939 her brother Menahem, who was living in Vilna, moved to Minsk: 'That is all I know about him. Nor do I know about the fate of my sister Eva who left Bialystok in 1939.'

When war came in September 1939, with the German invasion of Poland, Bialystok became a part of Soviet-controlled eastern Poland. Bertha celebrated her eighteenth and nineteenth birthdays as a Soviet citizen. In June 1941, with the German invasion of the Soviet Union, Bialystok was one of the first cities to fall under Nazi rule. Thousands of Jews sought to escape eastward, among them Bertha and another of her brothers, Ovsey. During their flight, Ovsey was killed by a bomb fragment.

German forces having reached Vilna and Minsk, no eastward escape was possible. Driven back to Bialystok, Bertha, her sister Maria, and her mother lived in the ghetto: 'The nightmare ghetto life began,' Bertha recalls. 'The synagogue with people inside was set on fire, the most part of men were transported out of the ghetto under a pretext and then shot down: inhuman executions.' Bertha was a witness to many savage crimes, passing her twentieth and twenty-first birthdays under Nazi rule.

In 1943 the Germans began the systematic 'liquidation' of Jews in the Bialystok ghetto: tens of thousands were murdered. Then, on 14 August, the date planned for the final 'liquidation', the remnants of the Jewish population, starving, emaciated, almost entirely without weapons, with no possible shelter but the cellars and sewers of a ghetto under siege, challenged the Germans to armed combat: an act of considerable courage for all those who, with no means or hope of success against the military might of a victorious Germany, felt that they must make their own gesture of defiance.

With the unequal battle over, the uprising crushed,

and hundreds of Jews executed on the spot, the Germans proceeded with the final deportation. Long lines of Jews, under armed guard, were taken across Bialystok to the railway sidings on which the cattle trucks were waiting. 'I tried to go into hiding,' Bertha recalls, 'to fight for my life, but after a few days, I realized that the situation was hopeless. When I came to the assembly place, I found that my mother and sister Maria had already been sent away.'

Bertha's account continues: 'I saw Dr Seligman in the train. He was a tall deaf man. While in the car he took poison and died. When the train started there were forty girls in our car. We understood quite clearly where we were being carried. Doctor Chernolesskaya from Lodz had a razor blade with her, and when the train approached Radom, we gathered all our courage and took the decision. Doctor Chernolesskaya cut the veins on the hands of all the girls in the car. I fainted but survived. Most of the girls died.'

Bertha reached Majdanek, where she was kept for several months. Then, after a selection of the 'youngest and fittest', she was sent to a labour camp at Blizyn, near Radom. At the camp she found fifteen girls, 'all that remained of the Czestochowa and Radom ghettos'. Then a train arrived with doctors and nurses from the Bialystok ghetto, the last of the surviving Jews of Bialystok. 'I remember Doctors Adomovitch and Knyarev. I don't remember names in this camp.' Later, all the young children in the camp were taken away from their parents. None were ever seen again.

On 31 July 1944, as the Red Army entered Poland, Bertha's labour camp was closed down, and all the surviving prisoners, 3,000 in all, were deported in a single train from Radom to Upper Silesia. Their destination was Auschwitz. More than 500 of those deported were taken straight from the railway siding to the gas chamber.

Bertha was selected once more for work, and sent to the women's section of the camp, for slave labour. On reaching the women's camp she was tattooed on her forearm, her Auschwitz number: A.15772.

Still able to work, Bertha survived. From the women's camp at Auschwitz she was sent to the labour camp at the nearby industrial town of Hindenburg. She was working at Hindenburg on her twenty-third birthday, a slave of the Reich. Then, in January 1945, as the Red Army approached Silesia, Bertha and her fellow prisoners were driven out, on foot, towards Germany. After several days, during which hundreds were shot, the prisoners were loaded into open railway wagons, and transported westward. During this train journey many more died of exposure, before reaching their new destination, Buchenwald: 'We were brought to Buchenwald more dead than alive.' But even in Buchenwald there was to be no rest, and as United States troops approached the camp, Bertha was among those moved once again, this time northwards, to Belsen.

In Belsen came liberation: the arrival of British troops in April 1945. 'I was dying of dysentery. I was in the hospital for many months, first in an English hospital, then in a Soviet one.' Bertha knew of only one surviving relative, a distant cousin, living in Moscow. She therefore left Belsen for the Soviet Union.

Bertha Sokolovskaya, the survivor, married in the Soviet Union a Jew, Grigory Shachovsky, a Muscovite, a well-known Soviet screenwriter, author of the scripts of

'Help me to realize my dream'

the films *Gavroche* and *Dawn in Paris*. Their daughter Alla was born in 1956. Grigory Shachovsky died in 1968.

In 1975 Alla married a young historian, Leonid Praisman. They have one son, Pavel. Four years ago, Bertha, Alla and Leonid applied for visas to Israel. Their applications were refused. Leonid, a teacher of history, lost his job. Now he works as a nightwatchman in a garage.

Bertha Shachovsky feels that she has suffered enough not to deserve 'to spend the rest of my life on my native land'. She also appeals for outside protests on her behalf: 'Don't be afraid to make worse for us. Our situation is so bad that it can't become worse. Help me to realize my dream.'

12

'People of the Spirit'

———◇———

Jewish religious and cultural activity in the Soviet Union is strictly curtailed. It is possible for Jews to go to synagogue. Like myself, many western visitors have attended synagogue services in Leningrad or Moscow, and seen Soviet Jews at prayer. In March 1983 a young Jew wrote to me from Minsk that 'there were lots of people in the synagogue' on the eve of Passover. But there are few synagogues even in cities with large Jewish populations. For the two million Jews of the Soviet Union there are only sixty synagogues, of which twenty are in Georgia, with a Jewish population of only 28,000. In Moscow there are only two synagogues in a city with more than half a million Jews.

Synagogues in the Soviet Union are forbidden to foster cultural, communal or teaching activity, some of their main functions in the West. Soviet synagogues are certainly houses of prayer. But they have long ago ceased to be, and are forbidden to become, spiritual centres.

There is no Jewish school, religious or secular, anywhere in the Soviet Union. Only two Jewish newspapers exist. One is a four-page daily newspaper in

'People of the Spirit'

Yiddish, with a print run of about a thousand copies an issue, published in the remote Jewish Autonomous Region of Birobidjan, where fewer than 12,000 Jews live. The other is the monthly literary journal, *Sovietishe Heimland*, also published in Yiddish, of which about seven thousand copies are printed, in Moscow. Not a single Jewish newspaper or magazine is allowed in the Russian language, although this is the language spoken by ninety-seven per cent of Soviet Jews, including more than seven eighths of the Jews in Birobidjan.

Unlike most other religious denominations in the Soviet Union, the Jewish religious community has been denied the right to form either a nationwide or a regional organization. No Jewish religious periodical or bulletin is permitted. Religious literature is practically non-existent. Jewish ritual objects cannot be manufactured inside the Soviet Union, and are generally not allowed to be sent into the country from abroad.

There is no rabbinical training within the Soviet Union. 'Even a wedding in a synagogue is difficult for us,' one refusenik told me. 'The rabbi is afraid to conduct the service.'

Such teaching as exists of religious values goes on outside the synagogues, privately, and under the perpetual frown of officialdom. Again and again these private religious classes are interrupted, or broken up entirely, and those attending are warned not to do so. In Moscow and Leningrad two young religious leaders, Ilya Essas and Grigory Vasserman, both in their thirties, serve as teachers and mentors to those who wish to study the Bible, or to learn the rudiments of Jewish religious observance.

It was at Vasserman's apartment on Culture Avenue

that the arrest of Evgeni Lein had taken place in May 1981. By profession a communications engineer, and in his youth, by reputation, very much a 'man about town', Vasserman was refused a visa in 1977 'because of the nature of his work'. After his refusal, his life changed. He became religious, devoted himself to teaching Hebrew, presided over meetings to discuss Jewish culture, and founded a seminar for the study of the Torah: the Jewish law based upon the Bible.

Again and again, Vasserman's pupils told me of the intensity of his dedication. His work was always done openly. He never concealed the date or place of a seminar, and it was open to all. Often under surveillance, he feared nothing. But the authorities had scant respect for such an attitude, and on 17 January 1982, on return from giving a Hebrew lesson in a friend's apartment, he was beaten up by three 'hooligans' in the street, and his face badly injured.

Vasserman continued with his teaching. Several of those whom he taught became teachers in their turn. One of his pupils was Evgenia Utevskaya, the girl who spoke up so bravely at the trial against Lein. 'Bible is the first thing that I must know,' she told me. 'It is more fundamental.' But she stresses that it takes 'a lot of courage for young people to come to the religious studies'. Utevskaya is only in her mid-twenties. She was born on 6 September 1957, and speaks as one who has been deeply immersed now for three years in the Jewish religious revival. The 'young people' for whom she has such sympathy are those who, in their late teens or very early twenties, will have their names noted by the authorities as having attended one of Vasserman's small classes, and will then be forced, perhaps, to leave their

Institute of Higher Learning.

Those who study the Bible, and also seek to lead a religious life, are not deterred by the constant harassment. Like the secular refuseniks, they have an inner conviction that their struggle is worthwhile, that it may not be in vain. The authorities can be harsh, but it is a pinprick against their faith. Recently, in Leningrad, the synagogue officials, who had hitherto lent books from the synagogue library, were forbidden to do so. This cut off the young religious students from a rich source of literature. But Vasserman takes the matter philosophically. 'Now the really strong problem is not about religious books,' he says, 'but for readers for the books.'

Talking to Vasserman, I felt the impact of his personality: his was the genial tolerance and good humour of a man of powerful convictions, not afraid to give effect to them, yet also undogmatic.

'Four years ago', Vasserman tells me, 'I came to understand that the only real foundation of Jewish life, whether cultural, secular or linguistic, is our Torah, our Jewish law.'

One of those who had known Vasserman before 1979 told me of the transformation from the young vodka-drinking student to the religious leader. 'In front of my eyes he changed – and changed, and changed – and became more and more striking in his conscientiousness. Now he lives not for himself, only for others.'

The transformation in Vasserman was reflected in the transformation in others. Utevskaya also had shown as a teenager no interest in religion, and there were many others like her. But, since 1979, 'such transformations of the people is unbelievable,' she says. 'All that you see is the result of the last two to three years.'

The Jews of Hope

Not only Vasserman, but his own friend and mentor, Grigory Kanovich, played a major part in this: 'A very good man' was how one young refusenik described him. Two years ago, Kanovich was given a visa for Israel. The refuseniks have a rule: when one of them receives a visa, he goes, however much his presence and his influence might be missed. Kanovich went, and several refuseniks have the photograph of his farewell dinner pinned up in their bookcases: much laughter, much merriment, and the raising of glasses for the one chosen out of the many.

A number of Kanovich's former students recall how his departure, as well as that of Utevskaya's father, Lev Utevsky, created a gap in teaching. But Vasserman carried on, bearing the burden willingly, holding his classes for all who wish to live as Jews, and to learn about Jewish law and practice. I was present in his apartment as a Bible class gathered: eight keen young men and women, most of whom had not yet applied for their visa, having as yet no possibility of applying, no invitation, no parent in Israel, or no parental permission, but for whom the chance of returning to Judaism was a precious ambition.

Vasserman is a wise and thoughtful young man, shocked by what he calls the 'deep lethargy, if not a dreadful coma' which engulfs the mass of Jews in the Soviet Union of the 1980s. 'Jews have always been a people of the Spirit', he explained in a letter to a friend in England shortly before my own visit to Leningrad, 'exalting elevated ideas and moral values and espousing them to other peoples inhabiting the earth. Now our souls are squaloring in the morass of the material. Not only are we unable to elevate ourselves above earthly

166

matters, but we have even forgotten that elevation is possible, that there exists a realm of the Spirit.'

'With my own eyes,' Vasserman writes, 'have I seen the results of several generations of assimilation and the experience was excruciating: alas, most of the Jews are willing to assimilate and are doing all they can to achieve that goal.' And yet, as Vasserman has himself seen on his travels to other parts of the Soviet Union, Jews continue to be affected by anti-Semitism, which he describes as a manifestation of the nationalism of the surrounding peoples, a nationalism 'which prevents the Jews from mingling with the indigenous population, whose main point is to eradicate the soul of the Jew'.

In many of the cities Vasserman has visited, he has found that the thousands of Jews still living there are no longer spiritually alive. In a city like Odessa, where he has seen the predominance of materialism, he has found that most Jews are not only indifferent to everything Jewish but hostile. He has discovered nevertheless, even in Odessa, 'the existence of a soul'. For he has found Jews there who are, he stresses, while few in number, still 'appreciating their Jewishness as their holy privilege, their honourable destination and duty'. In Leningrad, likewise, where he himself is teaching, 'I see eager Jewish eyes which reflect the soul's longing for Light and Truth.' Vasserman has made it his mission in that city to encourage the 'return of Jews to Jewishness', and to 'open the eyes of Jews to the grandeur of their own people and their elevated spiritual ideas'.

Now that the gates of emigration seem to have closed, Vasserman feels that his task, and that of the other teachers of Jewish history and culture, is even more urgent. 'Soviet Jews', he writes 'must *live* as Jews and not just be *called* Jews.' If Jews lose contact with their culture they will no longer have the spiritual strength to seek repatriation, or to identify themselves with the Jewish people either in or beyond the borders of the Soviet Union.

For Vasserman, to be a Jew means to be conscious 'of a line' between the individual and the land of Israel. He describes Israel as 'our eternal heritage, a land where from we were exiled and where we have always longed to return'.

For him, to be a Jew means 'not only to dream but to *do* something to achieve the goal of emigration to Israel. It also means 'to be quite loyal to the land of your habitation, even grateful to it for security, to toil for its welfare and still to live for the sake of *return*'. Any Jew who is not conscious of this goal becomes merely 'a person of Jewish origin'. Hence, in Vasserman's view, the importance of Jewish consciousness even for those whose possibility of emigration is for the moment broken. Even for those Jews who may never be able to leave the Soviet Union, who have had to give up all hope of emigration, or who may not want to go, they also, he argues, must be given the chance of learning about Jewish culture. 'Don't these people and their children need Jewish culture'? he asks. 'Shall we leave them to the mercy of fate and stop caring for them?'

Other refuseniks can explain 'refusal' problems: the search for documents, the application, the loss of job, the harassment, the uncertain future, the causes of hope or of despair. Vasserman sees it as important for him to tell visitors about the religious and cultural work being done for those who wish to exercise their rights as Soviet Jews: rights of worship, of prayer, of Sabbath observance, of festivals and of study. Sitting in his small apartment, hearing him talk of efforts which, although filled with dedication, are on such a small scale, I cannot help reflecting on the Jewish life here seventy years ago: of the world of Jewish theatres, of Jewish schools, of Jewish literature. Then, Vasserman and his teaching would have been a small part of a vibrant mass. Now he is an almost unique link between Leningrad Jews and their spiritual heritage.

Yet Vasserman is not entirely alone. In Leningrad his work of religious teaching is shared by several others, including the young Elimelech Rochlin, likewise a refusenik. All these teachers see in their work, as Vasserman expresses it to me, 'the way of returning Jews to Judaism'. In a world where Judaism has been for so long the object of pressure and neglect, this simple aim is in itself a mammoth undertaking.

In Moscow the brunt of this undertaking is borne by Ilya Essas. Six years ago, at the age of thirty, he began the risky task of teaching Jews their spiritual heritage. The classes had to be kept to a maximum of fifteen at any one time. Yet several hundred Moscow Jews have been through his classes. Most have remained practising Jews once they left him, their goal, to learn to be observant Jews, and, as observant Jews, to go to Israel.

Many of those whom Essas teaches become teachers in their turn. Some of his pupils have not yet applied for their visas, but, continuing in their jobs, they seek in their private lives to observe the Sabbath, to eat kosher meat – by buying a cow collectively – and to study the Bible, the Hebrew language, Jewish history and Jewish culture.

Essas, in his thirties, is both a man of culture and of

strong opinions, forcibly expressed. He sees Israel's strength as its spiritual stature, not its material success. He is a critic of Israel for what he feels was its excessive secularism in the first thirty years of statehood. 'No wonder so many Soviet Jews went to Brooklyn,' he says, 'when they could have two cars there, instead of one, and a bigger refrigerator – the things they were being offered in Israel.' The Labour Zionists, and the ruling Israel Labour Party from 1948 to 1977, 'they did build a building,' Essas comments, 'and nobody can say they did not do many good things, but they were not the people to put the light into the building.'

Essas wants modern Israel to put the emphasis on religious values. Only then, he believes, will Soviet Jews wish to go there in large numbers, provided of course their own understanding of Jewish values can be enhanced. A student of Jewish history as well as of Jewish spiritual values, Essas comments that before the First World War it was God's will that the Jews of Russia should go to America, 'to escape the Holocaust'. But now, he stresses, it is God's wish 'that we should go to Israel and to Israel only'. Those, like Essas, who do not feel that Israel is yet religious enough should, he argues, 'come and participate', in order to show their fellow Israelis 'what it is' to be religious. But Essas, much as he would like to do so, cannot make the journey on which he has set his heart, and spirit. For he, like Vasserman, is a refusenik.

In June 1973 Ilya Essas had applied to study at the Moscow Yeshiva – then the only officially recognized Jewish religious academy. He was accepted. Early in 1974, while a student at the Yeshiva, he applied for a visa to go to Israel. He was refused, and on the morning of 1 March 1974, intending to 'clarify some questions' connected with his refusal, he set off for the offices of the Central Committee of the Communist Party.

While on his way to the Party offices, Essas was seized by several KGB officials and militiamen, and detained. After questioning, he was warned not to go near the offices of high-ranking Government Institutions again. That evening he was released, and allowed home.

Three days later Essas was summoned to the office of the head of the Jewish religious community of Moscow, Efraim Kaplun, a Jew. Kaplun told Essas that he was expelled from the Yeshiva. 'There are no places in the Yeshiva', Kaplun explained, 'for those who want to go to Israel.'

In reply, Essas 'reminded' Kaplun that every year, at Passover, Jews recite the prayer "Next Year in Jerusalem." But Kaplun replied: 'And I recite "Next Year *here*." '

'I could throw you out *now*,' Kaplun told Essas. 'But I am a good man. You can stay until tomorrow. But tomorrow, go from the Yeshiva, go to hell from the Yeshiva.'

In the face of this treatment, Essas had no intention of remaining silent. 'I would like you to know', he wrote on 6 March 1974, in an open letter to the Chief Rabbinate of Israel, and to the Jewish Communities throughout the world, 'that the official leaders of the Moscow Jewish community prevent anyone who wants to go to Israel from studying the Torah' – Jewish law. 'But these leaders are mistaken. The Torah was given to everybody. It was given to the whole House of Jacob and to all the sons of Israel. Its light will reach every Jew who will place the Torah at the basis of life.'

The Jews of Hope

Essas was then twenty-seven years old, a mathematician by profession. His wife Anya was an engineer. It was Anya's alleged security classification that was the official reason for the refusal: three years earlier she had worked for a year as an engineer in a Government construction office. Both now lost their jobs. Essas, repeatedly threatened with the criminal charge of 'parasitism', found work first as a filing clerk, then as a lift operator, and later as a nightwatchman.

On 21 December 1976 Essas took part in the Moscow Symposium on Jewish Culture, despite warnings to all the participants not to attend. Some of those who attended, like Benjamin Fain and Mark Azbel, were subsequently given visas, and left the Soviet Union. Others, like Essas himself, Brailovsky and Begun, have been refused visas again and again.

As a result of Essas having attended the cultural symposium, his wife was told that he would be imprisoned for two years for 'anti-Soviet activity'. He was not; but he was frequently summoned to the KGB for questioning. Since 1973 he had been learning Hebrew and studying Bible. In 1977 he began to teach. Today his pupils, and his influence, are a powerful force in the Jewish religious and culture struggle. As I write these words, he is approaching the tenth anniversary of his first refusal. His father and mother were allowed to go to Israel in 1979.

On several occasions Essas has had books confiscated during searches of his small apartment, where the bookshelves are crammed with Russian and western books: Bibles, liturgical works, volumes on Jewish history and culture. Even in London, New York or Jerusalem, his would be regarded as a well-stocked library.

Essas expresses his desire to go to Israel, and the reasoning behind his desire, with continued reference to the Bible and its commentaries: the books that he knows so well, and teaches with such dedication. 'It *is* God's will', he says, that Jews should go to Israel. Organizations which work against emigration to Israel, or which prevent people from going, 'are doing something against God's will': of this he has no doubt. A Jew who decides not to go to Israel, whether from the Soviet Union or from western Europe or America, well, that is his decision. But a person who is actively involved in preventing others from going to Israel, he is a 'sinner'.

I watch as the young people crowd into Vasserman's small kitchen, themselves watched by his eight-year-old daughter Liza. It seems absurd that Vasserman and Essas should not be allowed to continue their studies in Jerusalem, or that their lives should have been made so difficult because of their spiritual beliefs. Yet both accept these difficulties without complaint. 'Nobody knows what can be dangerous,' is Essas' comment, 'and what will be dangerous tomorrow.' From faith comes strength, amid adversity, and amid growing uncertainty about the future.

There are moments when Vasserman is an optimist. 'The religious situation is rather good,' he says at one moment. 'I can learn. I can pray. I can help others.' But he cannot avoid the searches of his apartment, or the taking of the names of those who came to the classes. Nor can he receive through the post the majority of the religious books that are sent to him from outside the

Soviet Union. 'It is very difficult here,' he comments, now that there are what he calls 'new winds in life'.

Vasserman and his fellow religious teachers in both Leningrad and Moscow believe, from their spiritual perspective, that God opened 'the door to the Holyland' for the Jews of Russia 'because of his mercy'. But some Jews failed to use their opportunity of the 1970s, and went instead to the United States, while others were not allowed to leave at all, including those most highly motivated to go to Israel: men like Vasserman and Essas, whose deepening spiritual knowledge impels them to wish to participate in Israel's own 'redemption' through faith, prayer and good works.

As the young religious leaders see it, those Soviet Jews who went to the United States when emigration was in its full flood between 1976 and 1979 did so, in part, because they had no means, while they were inside the Soviet Union, of becoming aware of even the basic tenets of Judaism, Jewish culture or Jewish history. 'We Soviet Jews are very far from our national source,' Vasserman explains. 'And God closed the door. The Holyland doesn't accept accidental guests. It accepts only genuine Jews returning with the Bible in their hands and souls.' Such return through spiritual knowledge is, Vasserman concedes, a 'long, uneasy way': but he is confident that it will come, through the work of the teachers, and the will of God.

To be able to study their religious and cultural heritage, Soviet Jews appreciate letters and books from relatives and friends. But by cutting off correspondence, the authorities impede the free flow of materials. During an eight-month period in 1981, less than one in five of the letters which Ilya Essas' parents have sent him from

14 . *left* Anatoly Shcharansky in Moscow, shortly before his arrest in 1978 (pages 83–4).

15 *right* Ida Nudel (page 84) in 1974.

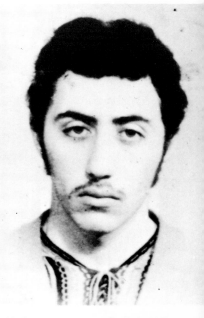

16 *left* Vladimir Slepak (page 84) before his five year sentence of exile in 1978.

17 *right* Simon Shnirman shortly before his second arrest in 1983 (pages 151–3).

18 Irina Brailovsky (pages 139–49), a photograph inadvertently released by the Soviet authorities because it was double exposed with the Henley regatta.

19 *above* Dr Victor Brailovsky in exile in Kazakhstan, early 1983.

20 *following page* Yosif Begun (pages 123–38) at the time of his second exile in 1980

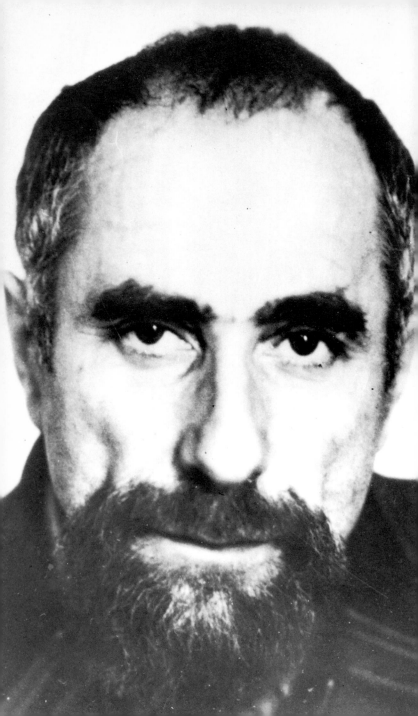

21 *above left* Yosif Begun and his son Boris in Siberia during Begun's second exile.

22 *above right* Ina Shlemova.

23 *below* Dr Yury Tarnopolsky (pages 207–9), sentenced to three years in labour camp on 30 June 1983, and photographed here during the festival of Channukah, on 16 December 1982, with his wife Olga and their daughter Irina, whose appeal to Mr Andropov shortly before her father's sentence went unanswered.

24 *above* Ilya Essas, refusenik and religious teacher in Moscow (pages 169–73).

25 *below* Grigory Vasserman, refusenik and religious teacher in Leningrad (pages 163–75), with his daughter Liza.

26 *above* Leonid Kelbert, film maker and producer of private theatricals (pages 192 and 206): a photograph taken at the end of 1982 in his Leningrad apartment.

27 *below* Ida Taratuta and her husband Aba, the 'father' of the Leningrad refuseniks (pages 181–8), in the spring of 1983.

28 *above* Evgenia Utevskaya's marriage to Sasha Yudborovsky, March 1983 (page 176).

29 *below* Mikhail Salman, stoker in a boiler house, formerly a medical student (pages 189–91).

Israel have arrived. For other refuseniks, the percentage of letters getting through, whether from Israel or other western countries, is even smaller. Many prayer books, books of Jewish literature, and other non-political books on Jewish culture, music and language, sent from the West by registererd post, have never been delivered.

The letters that are delivered are precious: Essas had proudly displayed in the front of his bookcase a letter from England with its large olive £1 stamp.

'Our little Jewish society here,' one Leningrad Jew commented, 'which is *very* little, it is under great pressure to be divided. The maximum we were able to organize was 1,300, at a festival, but that was the end of official tolerance.' It was also some while ago, in September 1980.

The pressures on Essas, Vasserman, and their pupils have given them a tolerance which is mirrored in the attitude of the non-religious refuseniks. 'The religious ones have become much softer, much more tolerant,' I was told by a 'secular' refusenik. And he added: 'We have got the knowledge that people still are different: just as in Israel. What is common with us is our desire to go to Israel – or to go to different places – to *go*. After great pressure from outside, we found the way to each other.'

After such experiences, my secular friend commented with a twinkle in his eye, 'it would be good for everyone to spend some time "in refusal". It would help him to adjust to Israeli society.'

Evgenia Utevskaya's desire to be a part of that Israeli society is intense. Her parents and her two grandmothers were allowed to go to Israel in 1979. Evgenia, then a student, remained in Leningrad, with her husband, Elimelech Rochlin, and her young son, Moshe, then aged four. For two years they learned Hebrew by themselves. Then they joined Vasserman's circle. 'He told me then he didn't know whether there would be a group or not,' Utevskaya recalls. 'Two years ago there was only one group. Now there are three.' She and her husband separated and later divorced. Evgenia was alone. 'Because I then had no one to babysit,' she adds, 'the lessons were often in my apartment.'

Evgenia wished to apply to join her parents and grandmothers in Israel. To complete her application she needed a graduation paper from her Institute. 'They didn't give me the paper. It took *two years* to get the paper.' Then, having applied a year ago, Evgenia found herself unable to get anything but a menial job. In July 1982 her application for a visa was turned down. For six months she was a street cleaner. Now she is a cleaner in a nearby hospital.

Evgenia's great-grandfather was a doctor in the Russian army during the Russo-Japanese War of 1904. As a result of his wartime service he was decorated for personal courage, a decoration which entitled him, although a Jew, to live in St Petersburg, then the capital. His great-granddaughter is, as it were, a beneficiary of this privilege. She may still reside in the city. But there the privilege ends.

In 1941 Evgenia's grandfather had volunteered for service in the Red Army in the Second World War, despite a special exemption as a scientist. He was killed in action in 1943.

On 12 March 1983 Evgenia married Sasha Yudborovsky, a young religious Jew like herself. Yudborovsky had been among those in Vasserman's apartment

during the raid of 17 May 1981, with Evgenia herself.
Some fifty Jews came to their wedding, from Leningrad,
Moscow, Tbilisi and Odessa. A few weeks after sitting
with Evgenia Utevskaya in her small Leningrad
apartment, I talked to her father in Jerusalem. He
showed me the wedding photographs, speaking with
pride of his daughter's courage after the affair on
Culture Avenue, and with sadness that he cannot see
her, her Moshe, or her Sasha, or greet once more her
teacher, Vasserman.

'We Soviet Jews are not politicians', Vasserman told
me as we sat in his apartment shortly before the start of
his next Bible class, 'and we do not know the way of
politicians.' He would like to see 'free repatriation and
free national culture and religious life: synagogues,
theatres, lectures, clubs'. Vasserman, like several other
teachers to whom I spoke, both secular Jews and
religious Jews, sees a delicate and important balance
between his work for Jewish cultural life inside the
Soviet Union, and the work of others for repatriation of
the Jews to Israel, arguing that it is the lack of sufficient
Jewish cultural life inside the Soviet Union that led to so
many Jews deciding, once in Vienna, to go to the United
States rather than to Israel. 'Jews go to America and
other countries,' he said, 'because here in the Soviet
Union they are indifferent to their culture and know nothing about their past. If they could be Jews by culture, and
not just by the "nationality" in their passport . . . .'

Vasserman, like Essas, sees clearly the link between
the right to study Jewish culture and to practise as a Jew,
and the motive to wish to live in Israel. Many Soviet
Jews 'cannot see Israel as their home', he argues,
'because they do not feel any connections with Israel and

its history'.

Vasserman also feels strongly, as do several other leading refuseniks to whom I spoke, that the emphasis in the western world should be less on the 're-unification of families' and more on the 'repatriation of nationality – the return to Zion'. Of course it is important, indeed imperative, that divided families should be allowed to be united, that Essas should be able to live with his parents and Utevskaya with hers, Shnirman with his father, Beizer with his son, Brailovsky with his father and brother, Ovsishcher with his daughter, Feldman with his parents, and Shcharansky with his wife Avital, whose exit visa was dated so as to expire within twenty-four hours of their marriage.

Such re-unifications are specifically encouraged in the Helsinki Agreement. But while there are many hundreds of divided families, there are more than 10,000 refuseniks without relatives in Israel for whom 'repatriation' is the sole hope. As Vasserman expresses it: 'We want to live in our own country and on our own soil, and to pray near the Western Wall.'

In urging that 'repatriation' become the dominant theme of a future solution, Vasserman sees no conflict between Soviet interests, western interests and Jewish interests. 'For the Soviet authorities', he explains, 'repatriation gives controlled, *unexplosive* expulsion. The emigration of the last ten years was an explosion. It was very fearful for the authorities. The repatriation to Israel is a more controllable process. For world Jewry, it is good that Jews can go to the Jewish State. For us, for the Jews of the Soviet Union, we can *La'alot*, ascend.'

———◇———

'People of the Spirit'

In their attempt to become 'good' Jews, and to prepare themselves for emigration to Israel, many Soviet Jews give their children Hebrew names. One Hebrew teacher whom I met in Moscow told me that in 1974 the authorities refused to register his youngest daughter's name, Rina, on the grounds that it was a Jewish and not a Russian name. He persisted, protested, and was allowed to register her as he had wished. One Leningrad refusenik sought official permission to change his name from Leonid, a typical Russian name, to Yosif. Permission was granted, and the name was changed on all his documents. Another refusenik decided to name his son Israel, after his wife's father. He was advised by friends, 'you will have to change that name before the boy goes to a Soviet school: it can only mark him out too obviously as a Jew.' 'No problem,' the father replied. 'We will be *in* Israel by the time *young* Israel is ready to go to school.' Alas, the father's optimism was misplaced. After repeated refusals, young Israel is now, perforce, at a Soviet school. He appears in all his documents as 'Israel'. But to save him embarrassment at school, he is known as 'Ilya'.

Despite so many setbacks the refuseniks live in hope. One Hebrew teacher, who remains a refusenik, was long ago given a suitcase as a gift from his pupils, in anticipation of his departure.

Against such hope, the authorities have sometimes resorted to an act of particular cruelty, the 'final' refusal: the declaration that the applicant need not even bother to apply again, since his request will never be granted. 'You will be buried here, beside your parents,' not in Israel, or anywhere else outside the Soviet Union.

These 'final' refusals, which have become increasingly common, are not justified even by the Soviet Union's own regulations. The Head of the Consular Department of the Soviet Embassy in London, I. Kuzmin, wrote to a British Member of Parliament, Neil Thorne, on 8 December 1982: 'In case the applicants are not satisfied with the ruling, they have the right to re-apply again.' But of what meaning is the 'right', I was asked again and again, 'if the answer is: "You will never see Jerusalem"?'

One such 'final' refusal, and a multiple one, was reported to the West on 10 December 1982. On that day a telephone message from the Soviet Union brought the news that four Moscow refuseniks, including the religious teacher Ilya Essas, and seven Leningrad refuseniks, among them another religious teacher, Grigory Vasserman, had been invited to their local Visa Office and told: 'You will never be let out of Russia.'

13

'Today it is so . . . .'

———◇———

A father shows me with pride the drawings on the wall of his Leningrad apartment. Most of them are sketches and paintings by his teenage son. One is a cartoon by a former Leningrad refusenik, Evgeni Abesgaus, who, in November 1976, was allowed to leave for Israel. The cartoon shows a calm, thoughtful, wise man, knowledgeable through experience, saddened through adversity – my host, Aba Taratuta.

Taratuta was born in 1930. He first applied to go to Israel on 4 May 1973, together with his wife Ida and their son Misha, then aged twelve. 'I have applied to leave now,' Aba thought to himself, 'so that even if we are refused for a few years, we will still manage to leave before my son is old enough to be called up for military service.'

Aba graduated from Leningrad University in 1958. He then worked as a mathematician in a Government office, and completed his Doctoral thesis. Before applying for a visa, he resigned from his post, fearing that his job might jeopardize his chances of a visa. But it was his wife's work that was in fact used as the reason for refusing them a visa.

The Jews of Hope

Ida Taratuta, who had studied languages at the Leningrad Pedagogical Institute, was a translator of English and American scientific articles. At no time did she translate 'classified' or 'secret' material. As an added precaution, she too resigned from her work before she and her husband applied to leave. Yet it was the alleged 'secret classification' of her work which led to their application being rejected.

Following his first refusal in 1973, Aba was forced to give up his work as a mathematician, and to take a series of jobs, first as a driver, then as a lift mechanic. No other work was open to him. Ida, who was working in a Post Office as a clerk, was dismissed from her job in February 1974. Twice more, Aba 'appealed and re-appealed' for a visa. Both new applications were turned down.

In December 1976 Aba had hoped to attend the Moscow Symposium on Jewish Culture. Instead, he was summoned daily to the KGB for 'discussions'. These 'discussions' effectively prevented him from travelling to Moscow, an overnight train journey. That same month he was told that he and his family would have to wait 'at least' ten years before they would be allowed to leave the Soviet Union. This time the reason given was that *he* had been engaged in secret work. This was the first time that this allegation had been made against him, rather than against his wife.

On 5 January 1978 Aba was called to the KGB. There, he was told that he had violated Soviet law and had been doing so for several years. He was warned not to talk to foreigners, and was told to sign a document relating to this warning. He refused. This refusal, he was told, was a further violation of the law. The warning had been issued, he was told, under an *unpublished* Soviet law,

'Today it is so . . . .'

'The Law Concerning the Declaration of Warnings', signed by the Supreme Soviet on 25 December 1972.

Aba asked to see a copy of this law, and was satisfied it was valid, although hitherto unknown to the refuseniks. The part under which he was cautioned concerned warnings for 'anti-social behaviour that may result in leakage of information'.

Aba still refused to sign any document forbidding him to talk to foreigners, explaining that he had left his job as a mathematician long before, and that even when he had been working in mathematics, he had had no dealings with classified material. He was informed that the Leningrad Procurator 'knew' of his case and that if it came to a trial, his refusal to sign would be added to the charge against him.

While her husband repaired lifts, Ida Taratuta remained at home, giving private English lessons. At the beginning of 1980, she was forbidden to use the Leningrad Public Library, under a new rule which stated that unemployed persons may not use libraries. In April 1980 the Taratutas' flat was subjected to a long search by the KGB, during which every book, every piece of paper, pens and pencils, their typewriter, the addresses of friends in the West, were all confiscated. Aba was told that he would be required to answer ten questions. When the interrogator refused to state on whose authority the questions were being asked, Aba refused to answer.

In 1978 Aba and Ida had decided to send their son to Israel without them. It was a particularly difficult decision, to face the prospect of not seeing their only child again. But Misha was then seventeen, the last possible year for him to go, if he were to avoid military service, and the possibility of at least a five-year delay after demobilization before a visa were granted.

Aba and Ida applied for Misha to go to Israel with his grandmother. But when the permission came, it was for grandmother alone. Misha appealed, but was refused a second time. He therefore tried to enter the Institute of Mineralogy. Despite his good academic record, he was failed in the examination.

Misha's failure was not an ordinary one. The deadline for an appeal was seven o'clock on the evening that the results were known. Misha's results were not announced until eight o'clock that evening. All the other students had been given theirs several hours earlier, with plenty of time for an appeal against the examiner's decision.

Not being a student in an Institute of higher learning, the time had come for Misha to be called up. But the actual summons never came. 'They kept him on a hook,' his father comments. 'They kept him in storage.' A talented artist, Misha took a design course. Then, in July 1981, when his course was finished, he received his call-up notice.

Misha Taratuta became a soldier, accepting that this could well postpone for many years his chances of a visa. But there was one hopeful feature. Confronted by someone so 'unreliable' as a young man who was already a refusenik, the military authorities posted him to a non-combatant unit, one where no secrets were taught or seen: hence Misha's hope that, when his military service ends, he will not be refused a visa on the grounds of secrecy, or of combat duty.

Of course Misha, like all those who apply for visas, must accept the fact that the refusal of a visa can cover 'reasons' which are quite unanswerable, such as 'inexpedient', or 'not necessary'. But he will at least be free of one of the most frequent of all reasons, 'secrecy': it is this reason which has held back his parents for more than a decade. Meanwhile, because of his artistic ability, Misha has been given work in his army unit designing and painting wall posters and slogans, work that he can certainly enjoy. Nor is he too cut off from his parents, who can visit him every two months or so, after what is, in the Soviet Union, a relatively short train journey of ten hours. Misha's military service ends at the end of 1983. Whether 1984 will see him and his parents in Israel is a matter which the authorities will decide.

After ten years of waiting for their visas, the Taratutas have stopped re-applying each year. As they see it, there is no point re-applying, since the authorities know all too well that they wish to leave. 'We have signs that they do not forget us,' Aba comments. 'The Civil Guards come from time to time. We are searched. There are articles in the newspapers about us.'

One of these articles was based on the 'decoding' of diary notes seized in the spring of 1980 from a British visitor on her fourth visit to Leningrad. She arrived in Leningrad on a Saturday. On the Thursday she was assaulted in a corridor, ostensibly by 'hooligans', and her bag taken. The result was an article published in the Leningrad evening paper on 20 May 1980. The gist of the article was then reprinted three times: in the Party newspaper *Izvestia*, in the Sunday supplement of *Izvestia*, and in the Air Force newspaper. This last reproduced the story in detective fiction style, complete with photograph of a woman with long cigarettes and dark glasses – allegedly the British visitor.

Taratuta's visitor was accused, wrongly as it happens,

of being a member of the '35s', the Women's Campaign for Soviet Jewry founded in Britain in 1971. This campaign, which has tirelessly championed the rights of Soviet Jews, was described in the Leningrad article as a typical 'double-dyed' Zionist organization, sharing with all other Zionist organizations 'the same dirty methods of a struggle against Communism'. Zionism, the article continued, 'is the child of one bone and one flesh of international imperialism, financial tycoons of the whole world'. As for Aba Taratuta, the article declared: 'Working as chief engineer he had access to the State's top secret material. Since September 1971, ignoring numerous warnings, neither he nor his wife has been working anywhere. This is also a certain consideration: to be tried for parasitism and then to pass themselves off as "great martyrs". Some people managed to pull it off: the Zionist propaganda made "fighters" out of those parasites.'

The article ended by asserting that, 'judging by the notes' of the visitor, she had 'got in touch by phone with more than forty addresses. And wherever she set her foot she sowed hostility to the socialist system. By flattery and lies, small presents and intrigues she lured the necessary people, ready for subversive ideological activities against our country, into Zionist nets.'

Not only does Taratuta's first name, 'Aba', mean 'father' in Hebrew, but he is himself a Hebrew teacher. Small groups of refuseniks, as well as those who have not applied or cannot apply, go to him for private lessons, and for moral encouragement. Some while ago, hoping to interrupt the language lessons, the authorities took away all Taratuta's Hebrew books: even children's books in Hebrew.

'Today it is so . . . .'

Although Aba Taratuta has decided not to re-apply for a visa, he still awaits the moment when he, his wife and son will be allowed to leave. 'If they want to let somebody go,' he reflects, 'they invite him to the Visa Office and give him permission, without a re-application and without new papers. They remember the applicants very well – thank God.'

As we talk, another refusenik couple comes in, bringing three tulips. Aba continues to tell his story. He is now a stoker, working in a boiler room. He has one night and one day on duty, followed by three days and nights off duty. 'I was lucky to get such a job,' he reflects. At that moment another refusenik comes in with his wife. It is five years since his first application was turned down. Then, he had been an engineer. Now, in his late thirties, he too is a boilerman.

Aba Taratuta's visa application was turned down ten years ago on the grounds that he had access to State secrets. Ironically, had he actually possessed State secrets, and gone so far as to sell them, the maximum penalty would have been from five to eight years imprisonment. 'So I would have been out of *this* country two years ago,' is his laconic reflection. Actually, he neither knew State secrets, nor had any intention of any form of anti-Soviet act or activity. Like so many thousands of his fellow refuseniks, his is not an anti-Soviet stance, nor a political one: it is simply the wish to obtain his right to leave.

Ida Taratuta continues to give English-language lessons to supplement her husband's low income as a stoker. Like Aba, she radiates strength of character which gives courage to the faint-hearted. But even she realizes just how irrational, and how parlous, their situation is. 'Today it is so,' she comments, 'but we don't know what it will be tomorrow.'

———◇———

Meanwhile, Aba and Ida Taratuta continue to lead as normal a life as possible. When summer came in 1983 they set off on a three week camping holiday to the Crimea, driving a friend's car, sleeping each night in a tent, staying for two weeks at Sebastopol – swimming, and eating fruit and vegetables to their hearts' content – before returning to Leningrad through the by-ways of the Ukraine and Byelorussia. In one of the towns on their return journey, Pereyaslav, they visited the local museum in memory of Shalom Aleichem, the Yiddish writer and humourist born there in 1859.

Their Crimean holiday over, the Taratutas went in August for a short visit to the Baltic town of Narva in Soviet Estonia where, at the seaside again, they were joined by Irina Brailovsky and her daughter Dalia. Back once more in Leningrad, Ida began teaching English again, while Aba prepared to return to his boiler house.

14

Luck and ill-luck in Leningrad

———◇———

A young bachelor breakfasts alone in the dining room of a large Leningrad hotel. Later that day I see him at a Hebrew lesson in an apartment on the outskirts of the city. He is twenty-six years old. Four years ago he received his first refusal.

His aim as a student was to become a clinical biochemist. At the time of his application for a visa he had begun to work on the early diagnosis of cancer, by means of testing the blood. From the moment he applied for a visa, he was thrown out of his studies. He immediately made a formal complaint against the Visa Office for 'the violation of his freedom'. His complaint went unanswered.

The young man's name is Mikhail Salman. His parents are both Jews. But like so many Jews of their generation, they had no wish to be a part of any formal Jewish life. 'At the age of fifty-five, my father has never been to synagogue in his life. Neither of my parents want to go to Israel. They want to grow old here.' As for Mikhail himself, and his friends, 'It is another generation,' he comments. 'It is another spirit. It is another time.'

The Jews of Hope

Mikhail is a great letter writer. He has 'pen pals' in Switzerland, Ireland, Israel, the United States and England. Sometimes he will spend the whole day writing letters, 'from morning to evening'. He estimates that he sends out more than fifteen letters a month: letters in which he tries to explain why he is a refusenik, and why he does not give up his search for a visa. Not all these letters reach their would-be recipients. But Mikhail goes on writing nevertheless.

Mikhail was born in Leningrad on 15 January 1957. Both father and mother were chemical engineers. For his first fifteen years he lived, as did so many Soviet citizens at that time, in a single room in a communal flat: himself, his parents, his grandparents and, from 1969, his sister Asja. A few years ago, Mikhail moved to a small room of his own in the centre of the city: a tiny room with just enough space for a sofa, a folding table, some bookshelves and two chairs. Here, an independent spirit, he writes his letters, reflects on his life as a refusenik, and studies Jewish history.

In the summer of 1974 Mikhail enrolled in the Sanitation Faculty of the Leningrad Medical Institute of Hygiene and Sanitation. In October 1979, immediately after applying for a visa, he was sacked. At first, he hoped to be able to continue his medical studies privately, by reading. But soon he came to realize that of all subjects, medicine was the most difficult to continue without practice and guidance. Some of his correspondents abroad offered to send him medical textbooks. But he had no access to laboratories, and no means of embarking upon experimental work. He therefore turned to his other love, Jewish history and literature. Like all Soviet Jews, he did not find it easy to get the books he wanted. But he persevered, and developed his own area of specialist knowledge, the ancient Middle East.

In May 1981, at the time of the raid on Vasserman's apartment and the arrest of Evgeni Lein, Mikhail was serving a two-week prison sentence for alleged 'petty hooliganism'. 'It was lucky for me I was not there,' he says, 'for I fear I might have done something loud.' But of the outcome of the raid he has few doubts. 'I think the Lein case was a victory for us. We spent the whole summer and autumn with applications and protests.'

In 1979, having been refused both a visa, and the right to continue his medical studies, Mikhail entered the refusenik road of menial work. In 1982 he received another refusal. Like several of his fellow refuseniks, he is at present working as a stoker in a boiler room. 'I am very lucky. I have eight shifts a month, so I have a lot of time to work *off* shift.'

Mikhail's main work as a refusenik is to lecture on the ancient history of the Jews, and on the Jewish wars with Rome. Three or four years ago it was possible for seventy or eighty Jews to gather in a private apartment to hear such lectures. Now no more than a handful can gather without the risk that some who attend will be sacked from their Institute or intimidated in some other way.

Mikhail Salman's 'Jewish' Leningrad has changed since he first applied for a visa in October 1979. At that time a Jewish cultural seminar was active under the guidance of Grigory Kanovich. This seminar hoped to give the Jews of Leningrad a basic knowledge of Jewish history, culture, and religion.

At first the seminars took place without any official action against them, despite several warnings to the participants to desist. But between June 1980 and April 1981 there was a more subtle form of official disruption when three of the four main lecturers were given permission to leave the Soviet Union: Alexander Kot in June 1980, Evgenia Utevskaya's father, Lev Utevsky, in October 1980, and Grigory Kanovich in April 1981. At the same time, harassment increased. In January 1981, after a lecture in Kanovich's apartment on the 'Compilation of the Talmud', the windows of the apartment were smashed by 'persons unknown'. In March 1981 Boris Devyatov, one of the active participants in the seminar, was imprisoned for fifteen days on the charge of 'petty hooliganism'. Beginning in April 1981 all those coming to the seminars had their documents checked. In May 1981 the Israel Independence Day seminar in Lein's apartment was stopped, and, when transferred to Vasserman's apartment the following week, was raided. At the end of that month a third seminar, to be held in yet another apartment, was prevented by militiamen, who simply sealed off the entrance to the apartment for the whole evening.

From the early summer of 1981 the pressures against the Leningrad refuseniks mounted. In February 1982 the young film director, Leonid Kelbert, who had given a series of private theatrical performances in various apartments, on themes in Jewish history, was imprisoned for two weeks. Shortly afterwards, three leading members of the Leningrad circle, Grigory Vasserman, Yakov Gorodetsky and Abram Yatzkevich, appealed to the Leningrad Municipality, and to the Leningrad Party Committee, to stop the persecution of Jewish cultural activity. The three Jews were told that they were trying to revive the 'anti-Soviet tradition' of the pre-First

Luck and ill-luck in Leningrad

World War Jewish Social Democratic party, the Bund, and that no 'non-Russian activity' would be permitted in Leningrad.

Vasserman and his two colleagues replied that before the Second World War there had been Yiddish schools in Leningrad, operating legally. This, they were told, was a consequence of the fact that 'Soviet Democracy had not yet developed its full measure – at that time.'

As the pressure grew, the young Jews of Leningrad decided to form a Leningrad Society for the Study of Jewish Culture. An organizing committee was set up, headed by Yakov Gorodetsky and Eduard Erlich. On 19 July 1982 the committee held its first meeting. About fifty young men and women had already asked to join the Society.

Determined not to break any laws, Gorodetsky and Erlich asked the Leningrad Regional Executive Committee to give their Society its imprimatur. On 2 September 1982 Gorodetsky was 'invited' to the Leningrad City Department of People's Education and told that his attitude was not in accordance with the 'moral image of a Soviet teacher'. Gorodetsky was at that time teaching mathematics at a city adult education evening class.

Erlich, too, was warned against pursuing such activities as Leningrad Jews regard as their preparation for life in Israel. Seized by the KGB, and driven off to a museum, he was taken into the room devoted to the Jewish Autonomous Region of Birobidjan, and told: 'This is where we are going to send *you*. Not to the Zionist-Fascist State, but *here*.'

'Would that we could all be sent to Birobidjan,' a Moscow refusenik – also a Hebrew teacher – later remarked. 'We could become Jewish again.' Such is the black humour of the refuseniks, the optimism of adversity. But the pressures mounted, reaching the attention of the Soviet public on 23 October 1982, when an article in the Communist Party newspaper, *Izvestia*, attacked the study of Hebrew, and of Jewish culture, as 'only fig-leaves, covering unlawful actions'.

This article went on to attack the activity of 'Zionist emissaries' reaching the Soviet Union from the United States in the guise of tourists, bringing 'instructions for renegades'. These 'renegades' had agreed to supply those who had sent the tourists with 'slander and tendentious materials' against the Soviet Union. Among the 'tendentious information' which the article claimed had been passed to these 'emissaries', 'through the renegades', was material about 'the convicted criminal E. Lein'.

Within a few days of the publication of this article, several Jewish activists in Leningrad had their telephones disconnected, among them Beizer and Gorodetsky. That winter, Gorodetsky was sacked from his adult education teaching job.

The Leningrad Society for the Study of Jewish Culture had no anti-Soviet or anti-Communist aspect. Its aim was to give Jews some knowledge of their past, just as every other Soviet nationality is taught, and indeed encouraged to learn, about its history. But the authorities would not accept this initiative, or this argument. 'Your Society', the organizers were told, 'does not exist, did not exist, and will not exist.'

Most of those who had signed the application for official recognition were summoned to local Communist Party committees, and urged to withdraw their signatures. They replied that elsewhere in the world, even under the most severe dictatorship, Jewish communities and societies existed. Why then, in Leningrad, was such a Society as theirs dangerous for the State? Only Arab countries, so the refuseniks argued, deprived the Jews of their 'internal' life. Even in the Communist countries of Eastern Europe, with Jewish populations 'hundreds of times smaller' than in the Soviet Union, such as the 8,000 Jews of Bulgaria or the 5,000 Jews of East Germany, or the 30,000 Jews of Rumania, 'they have their own cultural life, clubs, societies etc . . . .'

The authorities were not convinced. But, at the same time, they hesitated to declare the Leningrad Society to be an illegal one. 'Judicially our Society exists,' Mikhail Salman commented, 'because we received no written reply to our application for a whole month.'

Unfortunately, as all refuseniks know only too well, the gap between legality and reality is a vast one. When Gorodetsky was summoned to the KGB on 1 March 1983 and told to stop all cultural activities, 'or else', he resigned at once. Two days later, on Thursday 3 March 1983, Leonid Kelbert was taken to a KGB office in Leningrad and warned, by a senior KGB officer, that no Jewish cultural activities, 'legal or illegal', would be allowed. The officer also told Kelbert that whereas, in the past, such activities had led to a summary fifteen days in detention, as a 'mild' punishment, henceforth a 'criminal file' would be prepared, and anyone involved in such 'illegal' cultural activities could face the serious criminal charge of 'anti-Soviet activities'.

While Kelbert was being warned in Leningrad, I was in Moscow, preparing for my visit to Leningrad, hoping to meet Kelbert, and even to see one of his historical playlets. I was not to know, until I reached the city forty-eight hours later, that the pressures on Kelbert had been severe. We were not to meet.

In seeking to demoralize not only Kelbert, but all those young Leningrad Jews who have applied for visas to Israel, Kelbert's KGB interrogator was emphatic, that Thursday 3 March, that Kelbert had 'no chance' of ever seeing Israel. He had 'a good chance', however, of seeing Birobidjan, the Jewish Autonomous Region in the Soviet Union's Far East. The interrogator added that when in 1952 the Soviet authorities had moved against Jewish activists, 'perhaps they knew what they were doing'. That was an awesome threat, referring as it did to the last frenetic year of Stalin's anti-Jewish campaign.

In a further attempt to frighten the Leningrad refuseniks, the KGB began an intensive campaign on the dangers of passing 'secret information to foreign tourists', and making it clear that any reference whatsoever to the Jewish situation in the city, or in the Soviet Union, would constitute such information.

The young Jews of Leningrad have no intention of being silenced. Somehow or other, the cultural work will go on, and the celebration of Jewish festivals will continue. At Purim on 27 February 1983 at least three of the private celebrations had been stopped. But Passover, on 29 March 1983, the night of Israel's release from Egypt, was celebrated in countless homes. 'Practically everyone I know', one Jew reported to a friend in London, 'was either invited out or had open house himself,' while Aba Taratuta wrote to me of 'our holiday of liberty – Passover'.

15

The worsening situation

The pressures of March 1983 marked a new phase in Soviet policy towards the refuseniks. On the last day of the month, within three weeks of my own departure from the Soviet Union, the Soviet authorities launched the self-styled Anti-Zionist Committee of the Soviet Public. Some such committee had been nervously anticipated by a number of the refuseniks whom I had met.

The Anti-Zionist Committee declared that one of its aims was to show that Soviet Jews were 'an inseparable part of the Soviet people', and hence anti-Zionist. Eight pro-regime Jews were its members, headed by a seventy-five-year-old General, David Dragunsky.

Soviet Jewish activists refused to be intimidated. On 4 April 1983 six Moscow Jews, all of them refuseniks, wrote an open letter to General Dragunsky, one of the members of the Anti-Zionist Committee, and a Jew. 'What right do you have', they asked, 'to declare in the name of all the Jews who are Soviet citizens that they do not want to leave the Soviet Union? How is it that you have not noticed the 300,000 Jews who, in spite of enormous difficulties, managed to leave the Soviet Union during the last twelve years? Among them was,

197

by the way, your nephew, Boris Dragunsky. How is it
that you do not see the tens of thousands of Jews who in
vain are trying to get permission to emigrate to Israel?'

The Anti-Zionist Committee insisted that Soviet Jews
had no need of outside 'defenders': that their rights
inside the Soviet Union were such that they needed no
defenders at all. 'Yes, we need to be defended,' the six
Jews declared. 'We have no other defenders besides our
brothers who call themselves Zionists, brothers from
whom you want so much to isolate Soviet Jews.' The six
Jews added: 'You say we are an inseparable part of the
Soviet people. But we say we are an inseparable part of
the Jewish people.'

The six Jews ended their letter: 'We *will* struggle for
our return to Israel. We *will* be reunited with our own
people.'

From the city of Tbilisi, capital of the Soviet Georgian
Republic, a second letter was sent to General Dragunsky. Its authors were the two Goldstein brothers, Isai
and Grigory, refuseniks for more than twelve years, and
Isai's wife Elizaveta. They chose the path of humour for
their protest, asking, in their letter, to be allowed to 'join
the ranks' of the Anti-Zionist Committee.

'As members of the Committee,' the Goldsteins wrote,
they wished to put forward various suggestions for
action. These included a 'friendship society' between
anti-Zionists in the Soviet Union and in Israel,
publication of a list of former Soviet citizens, 'now
ardent Israeli Zionists', and a 'mass campaign' for the
study and propagation of the Hebrew language, under
the slogan: 'The better you know Hebrew, the better you
fight Zionism.'

The Goldsteins went on to propose a 'public

discussion' on the meaning of Zionism, with Yitzhak Navon, then President of the State of Israel, as their 'guest speaker'. At the same time, it was essential for a group of 'active Soviet anti-Zionists' to be sent to Israel, 'to give Israeli anti-Zionists help and advice'. This group, the Goldsteins added, 'is to be headed by the Goldsteins'.

Neither the Goldsteins' letter, nor that of the six activists, was published in the Soviet press. Like so much of the refuseniks' struggle, grave or humorous, it circulated among the activists, and even reached the West, but remained unknown to the Soviet public. But the 'replies' to such protests are widely circulated, and in an interview printed in *Sovietskaya Rossiya* on 19 April 1983, immediately after Israel Independence Day, General Dragunsky himself stated that Zionism 'not only rejects the moral values which we defended on the field of battle during the Great Patriotic War', but was 'incompatible with humanism in general'.

Throughout 1983 no week passed without substantial pressures and accusations against those Jews who wished to go to Israel, or who were active in the struggle to maintain some vestige of Jewish cultural activity and of Jewish identity. On 17 April 1983, two days before General Dragunsky's interview was published, eleven Leningrad Jews, among them Mikhail Salman, took a home-made Israeli flag to a picnic area in one of the woods outside the city, intending in this private way to celebrate Israel Independence Day. They were immediately tracked down by some twenty-five KGB men, arrested and questioned for four hours. Then, after the flag, and every piece of paper bearing Hebrew writing on it, had been taken from them, they were allowed to return home. That same evening they sent a telegram to the Israeli President, Yitzhak Navon, 'with congratulations on this holiday'.

Two days after this incident in the Leningrad woods the principal Leningrad newspaper, *Leningradskaya Pravda*, published an article covering thirty columns, denouncing the demand by local Jews for cultural facilities as 'nothing but a smoke screen for Zionist infiltration'.

One of those singled out for criticism in this article was one of the organizers of the Leningrad Society for Jewish culture, Yakov Gorodetsky, who had been a witness in Lein's trial. Gorodetsky, the article alleged, was one of those 'who treads the path of Nationalism'. Another Jew named in the article was Aba Taratuta, 'a tool of foreign emissaries'. He was abused for receiving a foreign visitor, in this case a leading western campaigner for Soviet Jewry, Lynn Singer, the President of the Union of Councils for Soviet Jewry in the United States. 'Of course', the article noted, 'we have to suggest that both of them were not talking about the unsettled Leningrad weather because she can't afford to waste time and Taratuta wasn't inclined to talk about the weather!'

The author of the article, B. Kravtsov, wrote of Taratuta: 'Don't be confused by his position today. He is a gas boiler operator. He used to be a scientist. He works not because he needs the money for food. It's only a cover to avoid being blamed for parasitism. He asked permission to emigrate. But he knew beforehand they wouldn't give him permission because his work was secret. He was waiting for the refusal and was very pleased he was refused! And why? No one before knew the name of Taratuta but after his refusal, he became a martyr in the eyes of foreign Zionists. Martyrs for the so-called rights of Soviet Jews and, of course, he is defended by American Senators and Congressmen. There are articles in Zionist papers and special representatives hurry to visit him.'

On the following day, in a sequel to this article, it was Grigory Vasserman who was under attack. He was said to be involved in a new 'psychological war' being waged against the Soviet Union, a war 'which is undermining our work for peace'. Vasserman, described in the article as 'a so-called authority on Judaism', was accused of conducting 'nationalistic propaganda'. He was a man who, according to the article, 'does not shun from shamelessly slandering our country and our policies'.

Aba Taratuta, Grigory Vasserman and Yakov Gorodetsky were described as being among those 'who toe the Fascist Zionist line'. The article added that the 'Purity of Jewish race and the exclusive position of Jews in the world and the unity of self-interest of all Jews is in direct opposition to brotherly unity.' The article continued: 'Lenin of course was against this.'

I myself was in Jerusalem when the first reports of this article arrived. With its direct attack on Taratuta, Vasserman and Gorodetsky, it seemed to those who heard it, former refuseniks, former prisoners of Zion, and those who have struggled to help them, to be another sign of storm clouds gathering against all Soviet Jews who sought to preserve and teach Jewish culture, to maintain contact with the outside world of Jewish thought or to go to Israel.

A further indication of Soviet intentions reached Jerusalem simultaneously with the Leningrad articles.

The Jews of Hope

It came in the form of a telegram, sent on 20 April 1983 direct from Moscow to the Hebrew-language newspaper *Yediot Aharonot*. The telegram was sent by a senior Soviet journalist, Victor Louis, a frequent spokesman for official Soviet policy. 'Whether you like it or not,' the telegram began, 'the saga of mass Jewish emigration from the Soviet Union has reached its end. In Moscow it is openly said: "The last train has left the station." '

According to Victor Louis, almost all the Soviet Union's two million Jews would remain in the Soviet Union. 'Recently,' he declared, 'there have been signs that instead of the movement "let my people go" a new movement with the slogan "let my people come back" is appearing.' Requests from 'dissatisfied emigrants to return' to the Soviet Union were all being rejected, however. Only if the request for a Soviet Jew to return to the Soviet Union was submitted by his relatives still living in the Soviet Union would return be allowed 'on the basic principle of a reunification of families'. 'It is therefore not unlikely', Louis ended, 'that we are witnessing the birth of a new movement of Jews returning to the Soviet Union.'

The purpose of Victor Louis's article, one former refusenik, now in Israel, commented, 'is to give the impression that Soviet Jewry is not worthwhile struggling for'. This will influence outside opinion to drop the cause of Soviet Jewry. Inside the Soviet Union, the pressures have been continuous since a speech by Yury Andropov on 21 December 1982, when, talking of the various nationalities in the Soviet Union, he expressed his opposition to the 'festering sore' of false cultural demands by 'bad elements'.

Andropov must choose, one refusenik remarked to

The worsening situation

me, as we discussed the speech in a Moscow suburb. 'He could let the "bad elements" – us – go. But it seems that now he would prefer to crush us.'

———◇———

During 1983 the attacks on refuseniks intensified in the provincial cities. In Odessa, on the evening of 4 May 1983, six people, one of them in military uniform, the others declaring that they were 'concerned citizens', entered the home of Yakov Mesh, a refusenik of several years, by profession a tailor, and an amateur boxer. A number of Moscow refuseniks who were visiting Mesh had their names taken. Several items were confiscated from Mesh's home. Half an hour later, another militiaman, who had brought two civilian 'witnesses' with him, searched the home of the Niepomniashchy family, taking away books, cassettes and tape-recorders.

At the age of twenty, the Niepomniashchys' daughter, Yehudit, is one of the leading lights of the Odessa refusenik community, a girl of courage and determination. Visiting the Niepomniashchy family that evening was a Moscow refusenik, Mikhail Kholmiansky, his wife Ilana and their teenage son. Mikhail Kholmiansky, a Hebrew teacher, was arrested on the following day, and sentenced to fifteen days detention for being in Odessa 'without permission'.

Following the Odessa raids, several local refuseniks who had been with Yakov Mesh on the evening of 4 May were 'invited' for questioning. In the following week, the Odessa newspaper *Znamya Komunisma*, the 'Communist Banner', described Yakov Mesh and Yehudit Niepomniashchy as among those 'dealing in Zionist propaganda'. The writer of the article, Svetlana Ostrovshchenko, declared that Mesh had committed a further 'crime' in receiving foreign visitors. During the search of Mesh's apartment, Ostrovshchenko revealed, maps of Israel were discovered, and also a photograph of the former Israeli Foreign Minister, Moshe Dayan.

Of Yehudit Niepomniashchy, the article stated: 'It is known that she invites young people to her flat in order to spread Zionist propaganda.' Not Zionist propaganda, however, but the strong spirit of Judaism, is Yehudit's unique contribution to her friends in Odessa. In April 1983 a cousin of mine, visiting Odessa, was struck by what he described to me as her 'incredible strength of character'. Asked when she and her family had last applied for an exit visa, she replied: 'We don't bother to ask for permission to leave. Why should I go crawling on my hands and knees to the authorities? I'm a proud Jewess. Why should I go crawling to them? They know we want to go.' Yehudit's last words: 'Stay strong for us.'

As the Odessa raids were in progress, a Kiev refusenik, Lev Elbert, was being threatened with criminal charges in respect of 'evading reserve duty'. Elbert and his wife Inna had first applied to go to Israel in November 1976. His first refusals were on the grounds of 'secrecy'. Later this was changed to 'insufficient kinship' in Israel. Yet it was Inna's brother who, from Israel, had sent them their invitation. Elbert's father, a wartime Soviet soldier, German prisoner-of-war and, after his escape, a partisan, had likewise been refused an exit visa since May 1980.

The Elberts in Kiev, like the Niepomniashchys in Odessa, have long felt the burden of official hostility. Both have been a focal point of Jewish cultural activity in their respective communities. 'Being accused of evading reserve duty,' Elbert wrote in a letter to England, 'I can't but mention that I have never refused to serve, but merely asked the Head of the draft board, a certain Colonel Rudenkov, to give me a form, stating that I shan't have access to classified information while serving in the unit. After him telling me that my application is mere poppycock, I've refused to take any call-up papers unless such a form will be issued to me.'

Colonel Rudenkov had gone on to tell Elbert that he would be trained 'for combat duty', so that if he were allowed to emigrate he would be able 'to fight against the Soviet Union'. Meanwhile, the Colonel commented, 'you'll suffer here'.

Elbert's trial took place in Kiev on 25 May 1983. He was charged with 'refusing to report when summoned for military service', and was sentenced to one year in a labour camp. That same day, in Vladimir prison, Yosif Begun and his lawyer, Leonid Popov, studied the 2,000-page file of materials on which, so they were told, the charges against him were to be based. The charge, they have been told, will be 'anti-Soviet activity'. The materials in the charge sheet include Begun's own concluding speech at his trial in 1977, and an appeal which he is said to have signed that same year, to the Helsinki Conference.

———◇———

At five o'clock on the morning of 11 May 1983, one of those Leningrad Jews who had been arrested while celebrating Israel Independence Day on 17 April was woken up by militiamen and taken to the local KGB headquarters. There, a KGB officer in plain clothes warned him that he was involved 'in anti-Soviet activity', both for the visit to the Leningrad woods, and for signing a letter to the Madrid Conference protesting about Soviet pressures against Jewish culture.

The KGB official added that the charge carried with it a maximum term of seven years in prison, followed by five years in exile. This was the possible sentence then awaiting Yosif Begun as he entered his seventh month in prison.

No week passes without news of the continuing pressures. On 30 May 1983 Isai Goldstein, one of the two brothers from Tbilisi who had applied to the Anti-Zionist Committee to be their 'representative' in Israel, received a further refusal for his official application for an exit visa. In addition he was told that he need not 'bother' to apply until 1985. Nor was his ten-year-old son given permission to join his uncle in Israel. Isai and his wife Elizaveta received their first refusal in December 1971.

To chart, even in outline, the day-by-day life of the refusenik, reveals the systematic efforts of a powerful State to crush the morale of the Jewish emigration movement. The individuals who comprise this movement do not threaten Soviet society, either intentionally or inadvertently. But the authorities act against them without respite. It was ' "officially" declared,' Leonid Kelbert wrote to a friend in London on 9 June 1983, three months after his warning to stop all cultural activities, 'that I would never, never, *never* be allowed to leave the country and, on the other hand, never (again never!) be allowed to continue my theatre activity in Leningrad!' His theatrical activity, Kelbert noted, was considered by the authorities 'as something between betraying my great country and espionage . . . .'

———◇———

The lottery of pressure, arrest and imprisonment is one without rules or predictions. The sixteen 'Prisoners of Zion' are part of a far larger group of refuseniks from whom, at any moment, others may be selected for arrest and trial. On 15 March 1983, within a few days of my own return from the Soviet Union, a refusenik from Kharkov, Yury Tarnopolsky, had been arrested, and was held in prison, denied any contact with his family. A month later, his wife Olga had still not heard either what charge was to be levelled against him, or where he was being held. It was believed in refusenik circles that he would be charged with 'anti-Soviet activities', in a deliberate attempt to frighten Kharkov's Jews from applying for visas.

A chemist, with a doctorate in chemistry, Tarnopolsky is forty-seven years old, fluent in Hungarian, English, Japanese and Hebrew. He first applied for a visa to Israel in 1979, together with his wife and their nine-year-old daughter Irina. Their request was turned down on the grounds of 'insufficient kinship' in Israel.

Having applied for a visa, Tarnopolsky lost his job as a chemist. In 1981 he became one of the tutors at an unofficial university, set up in Kharkov for the children of refuseniks by Alexander Paritsky, one of the sixteen 'Prisoners of Zion', and, since November 1981, serving three years in a Siberian labour camp for 'slander' of the Soviet State and social system.

On 1 October 1982 Tarnopolsky began a six-week hunger strike in protest against the repeated refusal of the authorities to let him and his family leave. He has never been afraid of expressing his feelings, or those of his fellow refuseniks. In an account of refusenik life, entitled 'Description of a Disease', he has written of how: 'Life stopped for us. We have lost everything we acquired during fifty years. We have lost our money, belongings, job, profession, skill. They call us traitors and double-crossers. We have neither past nor future. We don't plan anything, we don't strive for anything, we don't dream about anything except getting out of here. They keep us under the constant pressure of uncertainty. It is a real torture, indeed . . . .'

Tarnopolsky's account continued: 'We are the children and grandchildren of those who perished in the Tsarist pogroms, and the Fascist shootings, who were skinned alive by the Petliura thugs, and who suffocated in the gas chambers. We are the descendants of two victimized generations. We don't want to be the third such generation. We wish for the same things as all the people in the world do: to live better, to work, to rejoice, to raise children, to be happy. Most of us have, however, a very specific goal: to escape anti-Semitism.'

In June 1983 Tarnopolsky's daughter Irina, then aged twelve, wrote direct to Yury Andropov about her father. 'Respected Yury Vladimirovich,' she began, 'Not long ago, I came to know that an American schoolgirl, Samantha Smith, appealed to you in a letter, and you answered her. So I decided to write you a letter too. My father, Yury Tarnopolsky, is in prison now. He is accused of slandering the Soviet system and soon he will be tried. But my Papa is an honest man. He has never lied. He is under arrest only because we are Jewish and want to leave for Israel. Already four years we have waited for permission to leave. Now Papa is arrested and we don't know what will happen with us. I beg you to release my Papa and let us leave for Israel.'

Irina Tarnopolsky received no reply. Her father remained in prison. On 30 June 1983 he was brought to trial. As evidence, the Prosecutor stated that Tarnopolsky had received a letter from a former Kharkov Jew, Mark Pechersky, 'now living in San Francisco', who had warned Tarnopolsky 'to stop defaming the Soviet State'. Tarnopolsky denied receiving such a letter, and, from San Francisco a week later, Pechersky denied ever sending it. But on the following day, 1 July, the court gave its verdict, guilty. Tarnopolsky's sentence: three years in a labour camp.

In almost every Soviet city, Jews live in hope that the era of 'nil' emigration will come to an end, and that the pressures upon them will cease. But wherever contact could be made during 1983, news came of an acceleration and persistence of pressure which gave the refuseniks little cause for comfort. Pressures such as these are applied to many men and women who first sought to leave the Soviet Union in the early 1970s. Then, they were in their twenties and thirties. Their children were young. Now they are in their thirties, forties, and even early fifties. Their children are teenagers. Parents and children have grown old, and grown up, 'in refusal'. Hope has sustained them. But time has passed them by. Time itself, one of them wrote to me recently, is the 'dull privilege' of refusal.

The disappointment of those who may in their hearts dread the approach of old age while still 'in refusal' does not deter others, a new generation, from embarking upon the same road, seeking the same goal, risking the same disappointments. How well I recall my feelings as, in my hotel bedroom in Moscow, I held some twenty or thirty scraps of paper, on which were written names and addresses – some in Russian, some in Hebrew, some in English – of people who wished to be sent invitations, and were thus prepared, for their first time, to let the Soviet authorities know that they wished to leave, putting their careers at risk. The desire to live as a Jew, and to go to the Jewish State, remains as strong amid the new adversity as it ever was amid the old: a flame of national and spiritual consciousness that cannot be snuffed out.

16

Father and son

———◇———

The hot sun of the eastern Mediterranean beats down upon the low roofs and fills the courtyard with the sweet scent of orange-blossom and hyacinth. In the cool shade of an upstairs room an old man waits, nervous and uncertain. For four years he and his wife have lived in Israel. Their son lives in Moscow with his wife and young children, the grandchildren whom this old man has never seen. His son is Ilya Essas, the young religious leader in Moscow who first applied to go to Israel in 1973, and all of whose subsequent applications have been in vain.

I ask the father about his own life, but his thoughts and concerns are with his son. 'Write not about me,' he says, 'write about my son.'

The father's love for his son is evident in everything he says; in the deep sadness of his eyes as he speaks about their separation and recalls their past years together.

Zvi Essas was born shortly before the First World War in a tiny Jewish village in one of the western provinces of the Tsarist Empire. Between the wars this village found itself within the borders of independent Lithuania. Zvi studied at a Hebrew-language High

211

School in Kovno, and graduated on the eve of the Second World War at the University of Vilna, from the faculty of Physical Culture.

Shortly before the outbreak of war, Zvi Essas married. His wife Sonia, also from a small Jewish village, was the granddaughter of a well-known rabbi and scholar, a man to whom Jews came from all over Lithuania for advice and inspiration.

Shortly after the marriage, the Germans invaded Poland, and within a year the Soviet Union had annexed Lithuania. Zvi Essas' birthplace was once more within the Russian border, and he fought in the Red Army. During the battle of Kursk he was wounded in the knee and invalided out. While he was fighting, the rest of his family were murdered by the Nazis in Lithuania: all his brothers and sisters, all his wife's brothers and sisters, his parents, and his wife's parents.

When the war ended, Sonia and Zvi Essas, sole survivors of a large family, moved to Vilna, now capital of the Soviet Republic of Lithuania. It was there that their son Ilya was born in 1946. A gifted child, when he graduated from high school he was the only pupil to receive the gold medal for work of the highest quality. Later he studied mathematical logic, graduating with distinction. 'For a Jew it was very difficult to receive a high position after graduation,' his father recalled, adding with pride: 'but they took him into the Academy of Science.' Ilya married, and moved to Moscow to live and lecture.

Throughout his son's early life, Zvi Essas had been a schoolteacher. It was the Stalin era, when even the fact that he knew Hebrew had to remain a closely guarded secret. Between the wars he and his wife had lived a

Father and son

traditional Jewish life, celebrating the Sabbath and the Jewish festivals, delighting in the world of biblical recitation and inspiration. Vilna, the city in which they lived after they were married had always been a centre of Jewish life and culture, 'the Jerusalem of Lithuania', in which every facet of Jewish life found vibrant echoes. But after the war, it was impossible for those who had once known such Jewishness to pass it on to their children. 'We were afraid. We were afraid to give our son a religious education. We were like the Marranos in Spain' – those Jews who after their conversion had struggled to retain, in secret, their vestiges of Judaism. 'At our festivals we closed the windows and closed the doors, so that our neighbours would not know what we were doing.'

As a schoolteacher, Zvi Essas had to teach atheism and to behave as if he were an atheist. 'I had no right to be religious, I had to be an atheist.'

When Ilya Essas was seven or eight years old, his father took him to synagogue for the Kol Nidre service at the beginning of the Day of Atonement. 'On the way to synagogue I covered my face with my hat so that my students would not see me. It was not permitted to me as a teacher to go to synagogue. It was the only time that I ever took my son. That night, on our return home, he was full of questions. "Father," he asked, "why were the Jews crying there?" So it was that I related to him some of our history.'

The boy was never taken to synagogue again. It would have been too dangerous for his father to take the risk. But at home the boy learned from his mother something about her grandfather, the rabbi and scholar. 'She told him that he was like Nathan the Wise, a very clever and great man.'

In 1968 Ilya Essas, then aged twenty-two, found in the library of the Academy the twelve-volume history of the Jews by the historian Graetz. The volumes were in Russian. Every day he read and took notes. Then he began to tell other young Jews of what he had read; of the history of the Jewish people. When he had finished reading the complete work he said to his father: 'We have such a great history, the Jews. Why are we not told? Why did we not know it?'

Five years later, Essas travelled from Moscow to visit his parents. They were amazed when Ilya began speaking in Hebrew with them. Somewhere, somehow, he had chanced upon a Hebrew-language primer of a thousand words. It had stimulated his desire to learn 'the language of his people'. In six months he was fluent. He began to teach Jewish history and Hebrew to other young Jews. Many of those whom he taught were later given visas to Israel, when the granting of visas was at its height.

Zvi Essas, too, was allowed to leave, together with Ilya's mother, expecting that their son would be allowed to join them at any time. But it was only Ilya's pupils who came, with messages and enthusiasm: ' "Thanks to your son," they told me, "we are Jews. We are real Jews. Not Jews because of the word *Jew* in our passport, but real Jews." About twenty such fellows have come to see me.'

Zvi Essas had first applied to go to Israel in 1956, when his son was ten years old. Then, when he asked the reason for the rejection, he was told there was no reason, simply a rejection. But someone who worked in the Visa Office told him privately that the rejection came because

Father and son

he was a Zionist. Before the war, in Lithuania, he had
been a member of a Zionist youth group; for this 'I was
to be punished'.

Seventeen years passed and Ilya himself made his first
independent application. It was in vain. His father and
mother were given their visas in 1979. Father and son
have not seen each other for more than four years.

We sit in the cool shade, oblivious of the distant noise
of the Tel Aviv streets. Outside, the heat of the afternoon
sun shimmers between us and the palm trees, between
us and the orange-blossom. Zvi Essas has told me his
story and has fallen silent. I, such a short time earlier, sat
in a Moscow apartment with his son, walked with his
son in the Moscow snow, debated with him in a Moscow
street the current intricacies of Israeli politics, saw the
two grandchildren whom neither father nor mother has
ever seen, and Joseph, aged eleven, whom they have not
seen since he was seven.

I have nothing to say. I do not know how to encourage
a father at such a time. His eyes fill with tears, his voice
breaks, he looks at me in desperation, I who have no
authority and no power. 'Help me,' he says. And he
adds, almost in tears: 'Help me to be with my son.'

17

'Do not forget us'

In the course of setting down what I was told, or heard, in the Soviet Union, it has not always been possible to give the name of a refusenik, or to tell as fully as I would have liked the story he or she told. Almost all those to whom I spoke were emphatic that their stories should be known, and their names also, for assuredly I would learn nothing that was not known long ago to the KGB. But there were also those who were conscious of a danger, perhaps even a great danger, that their words might be used against them or taken out of context, and made a part, first of their dossier, and then of some accusation against them.

I was always aware that those to whom I spoke were not enemies of the Soviet Union, that they were not dissidents seeking to change Soviet society, and that they sought no change in the Soviet laws – only the implementation of those laws in order to allow visas to be granted. But however much I might say this, it could not protect them against allegations of disloyalty: allegations which appear with unnerving frequency in the Soviet press.

In order to protect those whom I met, whose names

might be used, wrongly as I believe, to impute anti-Soviet feelings, I quote in this chapter opinions without names: eleven comments which reflect the words, the fears, the hopes and the varieties of opinion, of tens of thousands of Soviet Jews who, as refuseniks, or would-be applicants, contemplate today, in their inner-most hearts, the possibility that their desire to emigrate from the Soviet Union may never be granted and that no one will answer their prayer: 'Next Year in Jerusalem.' One refusenik of ten years, now in his forties, expressed his fear that he would only be allowed out when he was an old man – 'too old', as he put it, 'to be of any use in Israel'. But each refusenik, so it seemed to me, was confident that in the end, by a process which could not easily be foreseen, justice would be done – Soviet justice – and that the exit visa, so long sought and so long refused, would finally be his: that he and his family would be allowed to leave.

------◇------

'The problem is action under pressure. Each day may be the last. You may die at the next moment; that, you have to accept. But you have to believe that you *may* go on for ever.

'Some can stand on a wheel for half a year – and do it well. And then they break, mentally or physically. They lose their teeth, their hair . . . .'

'We work against the resources of a big, big power. They can wait for a month, a year, two years. We have only limited powers. We have our own problems: personal problems: we are expelled from this society wholly. We hang in the air without any soil under foot.

217

'Since last year the psychological situation of many of us was very hard. To live under constant oppression; even without searches and imprisonment is not simple.

'At the end of October 1982, I was called to the Chief of the KGB, who said to me: "Our goal is to assimilate you, and people like you. You don't let us do it – you are our obstacle." '

'The Soviet officials say: "In 1970 we created the opportunity for Jewish emigration, which created the problem. So now we will close the emigration off, and end the problem."

'But it is impossible for them now. When a wheel starts to roll it is not quite so easy to stop it.

'Individuals, however, may break – and the daily strains are such that which of us here could say, "I would not give in." '

'Now is a good time to influence the authorities here, as they want to be in the good books of Europe. To demonstrate humanity – with people it has held in refusal.

'If they want to demonstrate their sincerity, the easiest way is with this problem. But how can it be achieved? It is possible to try. Here we are, a raw nerve. If they feel they touch it here and it responds in Europe or North America.

'Why not agree to a status quo? A continued emigration as over the past twelve years, but controlled? They don't have to break the norm, and so they don't have to explain it to people here.

'We will see.'

'Do not forget us'

'Good relations between the United States and the Soviet Union is the main thing for us. We must wait for the next United States Presidential Elections, for after Reagan. Now, after many years without emigration, lots of people have depression.

'The Soviet Union is under no pressure from the western countries. Oil is not pressure. The real pressure is Jews. The United States has Jews. You in Britain have Jews. You have a certain pressure on your Government.

'The answer to emigration is, we can increase it after good relations between the Soviet Union and western countries.

'People who get permission now, it is a very little thing. But it is still alive. These are the "Andropov permissions". If he continues to do a little, even if it is only a little, it means they have decided to *continue* their game, their play.'

'New people come. Old slip out – or go to Israel. Sometimes the most active must call a halt. It is not a matter of giving up, or of betraying: but of realizing that it will not give results any more. Those who do not understand this – like Yosif Begun – who would not stand aside, go to prison.

'It is a matter of finding a way to participate. The problem is to continue the activities. Sooner or later one may be pressed out of all activity.

'Last year, the Israeli President, Yitzhak Navon, said that there were two problems: first to create a situation which makes it possible for Jewish cultural activity in the Soviet Union, second to create a situation in which Jews can leave.

'But I believe such cultural activity has no chance

219

here. Just as Jews, we are considered by the Soviet authorities too dynamic, too flexible, too capable to accept new ideas. It can therefore never be *real* cultural life here.

'I am for cultural work here as an instrument, to present to the people very positive emotions and goals at a time of very great difficulty for emigration. They are meeting. They are gaining some internal basis, as a people.

'People who accepted some kind of culture, who fell in love with Jewish history, or Jewish life, or Jewish religion: are much more stable, can stand a much greater pressure.

'This cultural work creates a Jewish life inside the refusal movement. It creates the possibility to transfer information. We don't have an organization to act for us. Therefore cultural life alone has to create for us a mechanism: it is the only mechanism we really have.

'They will tolerate our cultural activity only if it then flows out of the country with our emigration. But if they close completely all emigration flow, they will crush all real cultural activity, except as a show.'

'It is a very big pain to have to bring my children up here; to have them go through what I've been through.

'We must demand that the authorities stop the persecution of people because they want to go to Israel. They said to me once: "We will fabricate a trial against you." Of course such threats frighten many people.'

'The KGB told a friend of mine: "We will not allow any Jewish cultural life here: either from your side, or through the Soviet Government. We will prevent your lectures."

'That is why I think emigration to Israel must be the first thing for us. The people here must have hope to leave the country – and to live as Jews. But we have so much difficulty to study. We have one volume of Dubnov's history for many thousands of people. If we photocopy it, it is against the law, and the people who did it can be imprisoned.'

'My parents' generation were afraid. It was the Stalin time. They tried to make Russians of us. We didn't know Hebrew language, the Jewish story. It was dangerous.

'But when emigration to Israel began after 1970 many Jews began to study Hebrew: and our children studied better than we.

'But now, after this emigration stopped, interest began to fall. It is a dangerous time returning. If emigration does not return, then this interest in Jewish history will fall.

'It will become dangerous again to lead the life of Jew: and impossible to continue without hope of early emigration. It will *never* not be impossible to be Jewish in this country.

'I think now the interest to Soviet Jews falls abroad. I am sorry. I understand every man from abroad has his problems. He is busy. But it is very important for us.'

'The cries from the West are our only hope. Here we cannot do *anything*. We will be crushed on the spot.'

———◇———

The Jews whose words I have quoted in this chapter, and the Jews of whom I have written in these pages, are

221

The Jews of Hope

warm-hearted, cultured people, wise with the wisdom of experience, and faithful to what they see as their national goal. They love learning, and they love teaching. They are kind people, whose eyes still twinkle, despite three, five, ten, and even twelve years in the cruel no-man's land of refusal.

I felt proud, as a Jew, to sit with them and talk to them. I felt strengthened by their courage and uplifted by their faith. But at the same time I was distressed to feel that we in the West may fail them, by not doing everything possible to give them our support and to make their plight more widely known.

Those Jews who have been refused permission to leave the Soviet Union have been portrayed as parasites. They have faced the full rigours of criminal law, although they have carefully sought not to commit any crime. Their courage and their hope has caused them to be made outcasts in their own society and hostages to powers and forces beyond their control. This makes their emigration even more urgent.

Back in the West, I cannot forget the words spoken by a young Leningrad Jew when the moment came to say goodbye for the last time. As the icy wind blew in our faces he remarked softly: 'Do not forget us.'

Epilogue

———◆———

In June 1983 I dedicated the sixth volume of the Churchill biography to Yuly Kosharovsky and Aba Taratuta, two Soviet Jews whose story is told in these pages, and who were then in their twelfth and tenth years as refuseniks.

In asking for a specific date when their visas will be granted, many refuseniks have been told: 'Never. You will be buried here, beside your parents.'

Such threats are intended to destroy hope. But the refuseniks are people of faith as well as of courage. In saying goodbye to Yuly Kosharovsky after our last talk together in Moscow in March 1983, I spoke of our meeting one day at my house in England. But he, as the taxi door shut between us, replied: 'You are invited to *my* house – in Israel.'

Index

Index

Index

Index

Index

Index

Index

231

Index

Index

Index

Index

Index

Index